PUBLISHER: AMAZON KDP
PUBLISHED: APRIL, 2019
ISBN: 9781092932561
2019 RONALD A. LAJEUNESSE: *All rights reserved*

INTRODUCTION

Every year in North America, over a million people choose to separate from an intimate relationship. In each of those years, over a thousand of those people die in violent confrontations with the people they once thought loved them.

All relationships have challenges. Fifty percent of them break-down, yet most people never even think about the possibility of it happening to them, let alone consider the consequences of deciding one of the most important questions in their life - should I stay or should I go?

Perhaps loving, long-term relationships are just not possible for many of us. Maybe they are "unnatural." On the other hand, maybe they really are as desirable as they seem to be and with the right approach, are quite attainable.

Is it that the idea of a long term loving relationship is naïve? Or are we not trying hard enough? Or have we not tried long enough? Is the effort one-sided? Was it that "she had an affair," that "we fight over money," or we "can't communicate anymore." There are probably as many reasons for the dissolution of a partnership as there are relationships and this book will help you learn:

- How to recognize genuine love
- Alternatives to marriage
- The significance of sex
- The differences in women and men
- The importance of where you live
- The consequence of culture
- The influence of religion
- The effect of laws
- The challenge of homosexuality
- The importance of where you found your partner
- The power of personality
- The effect of heredity
- The significance of a money attitude

- How to deal with infidelity
- The need to address addiction
- How to manage chronic illness
- Why seniors are now leaving long term relationships
- The potential damage from divorce
- The consequences for children
- The power of communication
- How to be sensitive to energy messages
- How to increase your consciousness
- What determines your destiny

You won't need to read every Chapter. For example, if homosexuality, illness or aging are not an issue in your relationship – just move on to an area of concern that is. In the end, you should have all of the information you need in order to make what will be without doubt, the greatest of life altering decisions - your answer to the question of "stay or go."

> Over the past 50 years the author has worked in counselling, college education, police services, health administration, business, private consulting, public school trusteeship and municipal governance. Throughout that career he has heard literally thousands of people lamenting their relationships and asking the question *"Should I stay or should I go."* Then recently he heard his fifteen-year old granddaughter Camille singing the lyrics of a tune of the same name performed by *The Clash*. One individual asks *"well come on now, let me know, should I stay or should I go."* Then the threats, *"If I go there will be trouble. If I stay it will be double."* The lyric is regrettably a typical scenario, far too often leading to violence and even death. Every year in the United States two people per million population are killed by an intimate partner. The Canadian figure is less than a quarter of that number, but nonetheless significant. It is increasingly obvious that the decision to stay or go must be made with great care as to "if," "when," "where," and "how."

CONTENT

Section 1: *The Foundation!*
    1. Love.................................. 05
    2. Sex..................................... 14
    3. Obsolescence 23

Section 2: *Why Them?*
    4. Searching......................... 29
    5. Personality........................ 33
    6. Homosexuality................... 46
    7. Heredity............................ 59
    8. Energy 66
    9. Consciousness.................... 74
    10. Destiny............................ 85

Section 3: *Universal Experiences!*
    11. Gender 92
    12. Geography 99
    13. Culture........................... 105
    14. Religion.......................... 112
    15. Laws.............................. 118

Section 4: *The Pressures!*
    16. Money............................ 128
    17. Infidelity......................... 138
    18. Communication................ 146
    19. Addiction........................ 154
    20. Illness............................ 169
    21. Aging............................. 176

Section 5: *Together or Apart?*
    22. Bedlam........................... 184
    23. Children.......................... 190

Epilogue: *Choices & Statistics*............. 198
Appendix: *Decision Grid*...................... 211

SECTION 1: *The Foundation*
CHAPTER 1: LOVE

"When you're in love it's the most glorious two and a half days of your life."
                              Richard Lewis

You met and married or cohabitated for this thing called love. Or perhaps you thought you found that "right" person who would love you unconditionally. Yet like most people, it is likely that you could neither define nor explain what love is. We covet this elusive thing that we don't understand and we refer to it all of the time. Most people will tell you they married for love. They will also tell you that they believe love is essential to a meaningful and lasting relationship.

But what else do we love? We are supposed to "love our neighbour." We love our children. We love our pets. We may say we love our home. Of course we love food and we may love our car. We say we love pretty much anything and anyone. In fact, the word love is probably the second most overused four letter word in the English language.

So what does the word love really mean? Interestingly, in spite of the many uses for the word, it's most intense and authentic meaning seems to be understood by children when we say we love them, or by a partner when we say we love them. In fact, almost all human beings crave being told they are loved and feel compelled to tell those they really care for, that they love them. Even adult children will describe how important it is to have their aging parents tell them that they love them.

But what are we really trying to say when we tell someone we love them? The ancient Greeks theorized that there were different forms of love and their historical writings describe four types that may still make sense today: Agape, Philio, Storge and Eros. In its simplest form, Agape love is described as a general kind of love that we strive to have for all of mankind. A kind of love that sees beyond the superficial dimension to the spiritual person within. Philio love can be described as a strong friendship. A love that is affectionate, warm and tender, but platonic in nature. The third form of love, the Greek's call Storge - the love that parents feel for their children. Storge is a love accompanied by commitment and sacrifice. Finally, they describe Eros, a passionate and intense love that arouses romantic interest and sexual activity.

Most of us have experienced all of those forms of "love," and perhaps in the absolute, each of them can be described as "true" or "real" love. Maybe they are all "genuine love," a term that is considered by many to be enlightened and progressive because it means "true, real and authentic." Perhaps genuine love is a combination of the Greek Eros and Storge forms of love – an intense feeling of passion, combined with a strong connection and commitment, providing reciprocal benefit along with some sacrifice. Love relationships inevitably begin with strong feelings that we might call love, but in reality may just be lust. The feelings are intense and powerful all right, but if we are honest, they are initially based mostly on energy and chemistry and they are assuredly mostly sexual in nature.

Psychologists will tell us that it is common for teenagers to confuse love with lust, but many adults do the same. In fact, if we watch contemporary movies or read magazines we will see that love and sex are viewed as one package. And perhaps they are; but there is more to it than that. Perhaps love and lust are not opposites as some authors would profess, but rather, related. Perhaps lust is the first stage of love. Not that we might love everyone we have lusted for, but rather it is the beginning of what could be love. Certainly it is a story that many a young man has told his "date."

Poets, authors and spiritual leaders have tried to define love for centuries and now scientists are trying. It is surprising that medical science has taken so long, because it is pretty evident to everyone who has felt the emotions related to love, that there is a strong physical reaction. That racing heart, the flushed cheeks, the unwanted perspiration and the clammy hands. Inside the body, estrogen (women) and testosterone (men and women) runs rampant. The twice a day sex.

We call it "love struck!" Scientists call it "monoamines," the secretion of extra dopamine, norepinephrine (adrenalin) and serotonin that give the participants a natural high. As relationships grow, additional chemicals play a role. Oxytocin is released by the hypothalamus gland in the brain of both sexes during orgasm and some scientists believe that it promotes intimacy and bonding. It is also released during child-birth, probably for the same reason, to help cement a bond between mother and child. We may see the following statement as good or bad news, but the theory goes that the more sex a couple has, the deeper their bond becomes.

As we can see, romanticists, authors and poets have tried to convince us that the heart is the center of love, but in actuality, it is probably the brain. The supreme emotion of love affects everything we feel, think, do and become, affecting not only our brains, but our bodies too - right to the cellular level. Science also tells us that we are all energy fields, that we are affected by, and that we affect those around us through our energy vibrations. We feel the presence - the energy - of people and events every day. This theory suggests that we are attracted to those who vibrate at the same frequency as we do, or we may feel rebuffed by those whose energy does not match ours. With all of this vibrating and element release, one could say that at least in the early stages of a relationship we are at the mercy of our body's chemistry, that love is driven by our genetic make-up.

But spiritual leaders see love from a somewhat different perspective. They will tell us that they know both from the scriptures and intuitively, that attaining love is a major purpose for living and that a strong loving connection with others is essential to all that we find meaningful. Some argue that without love, we cannot even survive as a species. Millions look to religion for guidance on how to live in a loving relationship and although churches vary in their structure and portrayal of their beliefs, if we look below the surface, there are many similarities. They all articulate beliefs that should support a strong marriage or partnership. They all profess to bring comfort and happiness to their people, they all have initiatives to reduce suffering, they all teach moral precepts and they all hold "love" to be the ideal state.

But religions often don't help, in part because people are asked to adhere to beliefs and affirmations without knowing anything about the underlying reasoning. They also do not help if what they say and do are quite different. For example, they hardly demonstrate unconditional love when their God meets out harsh punishment such as eternal damnation when "He" is offended. All of the world's religions were founded on a concept of unifying people in a caring environment, but then most of them declare preeminence and even promote their supremacy, using fear and violence to urge others to see the world "their way." That is hardly wholesome modeling for people searching for tools to build a lasting unified relationship on a foundation of love.

So if religion and science don't have all of the answers, where do we look for a demonstration of what love really is? A love that must be "genuine love" and not the love of a hamburger. Perhaps the answer is within our own experience. If we think about the early stages of what we thought was a real love relationship - assuming we have had one - or perhaps we have observed one, or simply imagined what one should be like, there was or would be much more than a physical attraction. There is that physical attraction to be sure, where we, or they, as the case may be, had trouble staying out of bed. But as the relationship grows, there is an intense caring. Loving partners want nothing more than to make the other person happy. There is usually a desire to surrender the whole self to a person who is trusted and expected to return the caring in equal portions.

In this form of love there is a vested interest in one another's happiness. People in love say they can be more of who they truly are and they describe a greater serenity when in their loving partners company. Love is not about jealousy, competition, impressing or changing the other person. And it is certainly not about manipulation, control or violence. Nor is it about being perfect. People in love may have as many conflicts as those who are not in love, but the difference will be in the caring they have for one another and therefore how they resolve the conflict. For example, jealousy will be fleeting and replaced by trust. Disagreements will not include hurtful personal attacks and will usually be solved quickly.

Although there are many definitions and many uses for the word love, the true meaning seems to be quite understood within a close relationship, perhaps because of the emotion and energy that accompanies the declaration. The love feeling is not necessarily logical or rational, but it is compelling. It would probably have been a good idea for everyone to have looked closely as a relationship began to develop in order to give some sober second thought as to whether one was feeling lust, love or something else entirely.

So what are the essential pieces of genuine love? The answer is within three "a" words. Genuine love contains the components of attraction, attachment and assurance. The first reaction in most continuing relationships is attraction. Some people say their attraction was as simple as scent, but whatever the medium, the result is the stimulation of strong feelings. Without the chemistry, without the compatible energy, without a catalyst for greater sharing of who the parties are, it is rare that any couple will want to invest the time and energy necessary for the relationship to move to the next level.

In genuine love, attraction is followed by an attachment, not unlike a parent-child attachment. If an attachment doesn't materialize, the attraction that was thought to be love, can be branded as lust. Attachment comes with wanting as much or more for the other human being than we wish for ourselves. In this case though, our partner feels the same way and the relationship is not about sacrifice as it is with a child. As we support, care and share the details of who we are within an accepting and understanding environment, the self-revealing behavior - when reciprocated - forms a stronger emotional bond and people merge closer and closer together. This movement towards intimacy is a crucial component of all relationships if they are to grow stronger and deeper.

As the attachment becomes more robust, the couple moves to a stage where they feel a certain security or "assurance" about the depth of the relationship. This third component reflects a belief that a partner cares for us intensely and will support us no matter what the circumstances. People who are strongly committed to one another will see the positive in each other, will want the best for their partner and will act accordingly, resulting in the building of a strong trusting relationship. The couple will then feel an intimacy reflective of genuine love.

Attraction, attachment and assurance. Like our formal early education, these "A's" will help us get to where we want to go. They don't however, guarantee long term success in a partnership, just as some "A" students never do excel. The "A's" can though, give us a better start. "Living happily ever after" is a myth, a misleading message about expecting the universe to give us the best without any need for us to work at it. While there are never guarantees, our opportunities will be much better with an "A" foundation than if we had built that base on three "D's" - deceit, dishonesty and distrust. Those that have "d's" in their initial experience can never expect much better from the relationship than a "c," corrections and consequences.

What is the foundation of your relationship? Beyond the attraction, did you feel a genuine attachment? Did you feel some assurance about the depth of the relationship? Do you now? Would you say you were in love? Are in love? Still unsure about love?

CHAPTER 2: SEX

"Among men, sex sometimes results in intimacy; among women, intimacy sometimes results in sex."
                    Barbara Cartland

In the past, most people would have agreed with Ms. Cartland, claiming that men believed sex was much more important than intimacy. However, recent polls indicate that while there may still be a hint of truth to the claim, what matters most to both genders is that the couple shares the same degree of feeling and sexual interest. While it may be unlikely that two people will have identical motivations and completely agree on sexual values, there does need to be a high degree of compatibility. Things will vary over time of course, such as during the hormonal cycles of either partner where increased or decreased interest may fluctuate. Interest also tends to diminish as people age.

To some degree today, but certainly in past generations, men were taught that sexual prowess was highly desirable, while women were taught that sexual modesty was preferable. Any degree of sexual prowess made women "slutty" and unappealing. These societal attitudes were then likely to influence the frequency and importance of sex in a marriage. For example, men might have felt slighted if their advances weren't responded to, while women might have felt pressured to have more sex than they were comfortable with.

Young women were often counseled to use sex as a source of reward, or as a weapon in order to influence their partner's behavior. Conversely men were taught that women should "honor and obey" and that meant, "sex on demand." To be turned down was a direct challenge to the man's masculinity and male ego, resulting in either feelings of being inadequate, or being a victim who wasn't receiving his due. In combination with these attitudes, talking about sex was taboo, so how were couples ever to resolve their differences?

In recent years the discussion of sexual issues and concerns has become more prominent and explicit in books, movies and within the home. In addition, most young women are far less restrained and young men are finding that their "feminine side" is more socially acceptable. The positive side of this new openness is an improved willingness for partners to talk about their desires and differences and there are often many. Differences that come from various sources like religious values, life teachings, life experiences, trauma, genetics and even gender. Women for example may demand more physical affection that may have nothing to do with wanting more sex.

While many men have similar needs, they are less likely to admit them openly. Men are also more likely to interpret affection as an encouragement to have sex. And it might be. But it might also not be. There are also biological differences such as the time it takes to achieve orgasm. On average, a man will take four to ten minutes while the woman may take up to 13 minutes. There are of course techniques and even commercial products to help equalize those differences, but open communication is critical to having them work.

So how important is sex to a relationship? The answer is quite individual and comes down to a number of personal and spiritual beliefs. Notwithstanding this truism, sex for most is a vital part of a meaningful relationship. Sex can be casual and superficial, but within an authentic relationship it requires a deep level of communication where couples are more inclined to talk to each other about intimate emotional issues, including lovemaking preferences. To be intimate and divulging requires couples to be vulnerable, which in turn leads to a deeper level of acceptance and trust. This unique connection that lovers enjoy creates a vibrancy and passion that probably can't be created in any other way.

As a general rule a "low sex" marriage is frequently a recipe for problems, particularly if the individuals have different values and needs. If one spouse is yearning for more touch, physical closeness and more sex and their partner has no interest, a major "disconnect" occurs and intimacy at all levels is likely to diminish. When intimacy disappears, feelings of being unloved, unwanted and unappreciated are likely to fill the void. It will then be inevitable that less time will be spent together, fewer opportunities for fun will emerge and the relationship will be at risk for dissolution.

So if sex is important to a healthy relationship, how much of it should we experience? Statistically, a number of studies have concluded that on average, taking all ages into account, married couples in North America have sex twice a week, more than double that of the single person, but less than their European counterparts. If twice a week is the norm, is twice a week also the ideal? Actually it probably doesn't matter because frequency doesn't necessarily indicate a healthy relationship at all. Sex in a relationship is only as important as it is to the individuals in that relationship and in truth, frequency is not as important as quality, because quality requires mutual respect, trust and open and honest communication. It is therefore arguable that for most people, sex is an essential part of a healthy relationship.

It is true that over time, many couples fall into a place of mutual comfort, where sex no longer plays a major role in their lives. Conversely, some couples keep the "magic" alive well into their seventies and beyond. They know and appreciate that sexual expression is an inherent and pleasurable experience with many benefits. The healthy sex life is quite simply a part of living, loving and growing together.

Sexual problems within partnerships including marriage, usually begins long before the decision to live together. When couples believe in the myths of "happily ever after" or "love conquers all," problems in the marital relationship usually surface within a short time. The belief that sex should be avoided until after marriage is often accompanied by a view that the topic is not even to be discussed. Those values often sabotage any future chance of sexual satisfaction and marital health.

There are of course many issues for new couples to deal with, things like finances, conflict, parenting, in-laws, leisure time, family and so on. And at the top of the list is sex. In the past, more so than today, new couples were rarely advised to talk about those matters. They then had no communication, no experience and no opportunity to learn for themselves, or for their partner. But why would they need to? Marriage of course was about living "happily ever after?"

Medical researcher tells us that healthy sex has many benefits from enjoyment to intimacy and stress reduction to longevity. For many people, sex to a relationship is like nutrients to a plant; it is essential to keeping it alive. Loving sex contains passion, affection, exhilaration and calm. So why does sex become a casualty in so many relationships? The answers are legion! The first is a lack of knowledge of one's own sexuality and that of one's partner. Even with early positive sexual experiences and an emotionally open relationship, sexual involvements can still become a casualty over time. Unless people do find frequent private time to talk about sex, they can be married for years without ever experiencing what is most exciting in bed. The older generations in particular tend to feel uncomfortable and embarrassed talking about their sexual needs and desires. Add to that a chance of exposing a secret wish and they introduce an intense fear of revealing an unacceptable part of who they are.

Then comes fatigue. Modern life is very busy and in many homes both mom and dad work at jobs and careers. A little fantasy or encouragement can trump most fatigue and after a great orgasm and a long deep sleep, or sometimes even after a short nap, people will find themselves relaxed yet re-energized. The third factor is boredom. Routine, family demands, repairs, bills and the lack of fun can take its toll. Then we have cultural and religious differences that can lead to misunderstandings, unshared values and conflict. Have you made loving sex a priority in your relationship?"

Many couples let the demands that seem urgent trump the important things in life. Or they consume too much alcohol, stimulating the libido, but hampering performance. Or they never alter their routine with something like a "quickie" when there is little time, or a "risky" in a semi-public place, or a full romantic evening, or a sincere apology after a fight. It may be a mistake not to plan a date night, flowers, or an evening away from the children in a motel, campsite or just under the stars. Unless one of the parties has a dislike of surprises, planning something new, different and unique can be exhilarating and passion producing.

The options are only limited by one's imagination, but experimentation in the bedroom takes a degree of risk and openness. Sexual toys, lubricants, erotic films, games and sharing fantasies can all have a place in spicing up a relationship - if they are not considered offensive by either party.

In some situations, there are medical conditions and/or medications that lead to changes in sex drive. Or there are simple attitude shifts in one of the partners that lead to changes in sexual values and behaviors. And the aging process will in most situations reduce the frequency of interest in sex. Even more difficult to address are sexual problems related to cultural and religious differences or a medical condition.

A sexless relationship is usually a problem, although it is recognized that in rare situations such as illness or injury, a complete sexual experience may not be possible. The bottom line is that it is always best to have whatever sexual involvement you can manage.

Pharmaceutical aids like Viagra or Cialis can be helpful, but only if the interest in sex remains active and the problem lies within the physiology of maintaining an erection.

There are of course "irreconcilable differences" where the couple can agree on virtually nothing, a sure sign that errors of choice were made very early in the relationship. In some cases, deep-seated psychological problems stemming from past traumatic experiences like sexual assault - if unresolved - emerge in later life and negatively influence relationships. In other situations, a death, job loss, financial difficulty or an "affair," can lead to disinterest and sexual withdrawal.

During every relationship, the magic may fade, unknown traits may be exposed and partners may take each other for granted. Not an unusual experience, but one that can send a couple down the road to separation, when the only trip they should take is to a bedroom.

Did you plan to live together before any knowledge and experience in the bedroom? Do you assume you know everything about your partner's sexual interests? Are you judgmental? Do you discuss the range of sexual practices that you are both willing to try? Do you try different things to spice up your life? Do you have ground rules that include either party having a "veto power?" Do you honor differing values and respect medical conditions? Do you find private time with your partner to talk openly and honestly about frustrations, anger, anxiety, disappointment and sadness? Do you talk even more frequently about the meaning of life, about goals, about fun, about the appreciation of each other - and about sex?

CHAPTER 3: OBSOLESCENCE

"According to a new survey, people who get divorced die early. People who stay married live longer. The difference is they just wish they were dead."
                    David Letterman

Two thousand years ago the world was ruled by Rome. From England to Africa, one in four people lived under Roman law – and brutality. The average life span for women was twenty-two, with many of them dying in childbirth. The average life span for men was twenty-five, with many dying in battle. The average age for marriage was sixteen. On average then, most marriages lasted under ten years.

In contrast, in the 1950's, North Americans married on average at age 25 (women) and 29 (men). That dropped to age 23 and 25 in the 60's and 70's, but is now back up to 29 and 31. Many people will live into their 90's, with an average life expectancy of 80 for women and 77 for men in the U.S. and 85 for women and 83 for men in Canada. All of which leaves us with the potential of living with the same partner for some fifty years and more. Perhaps it is not surprising that more and more partners are opting out of that scenario.

It also appears from the statistics that we have a society of half-hearted, semi-happy marriages. Studies report that many couples that don't divorce, trade in passion for low-stress arrangements that center on their children. These couples are by no means miserable, with the participants usually being friendly and supportive, but the ultimate result is a general dissatisfaction with life and fantasies about what might have been.

A recent survey done in association with Time magazine found that nearly four in 10 Americans think marriage is becoming obsolete. That's an 11 percent jump since 1978, when Time asked the same question. Another study found that those numbers increased with youth, with 50 percent of younger Americans believing that marriage is becoming obsolete because it has little to offer; that it adds nothing to life that a single person doesn't already have. Young people also look around and see the "control and loss of freedom," that married men report and the "loneliness" that married women appear to experience.

Many of these young people are now opting for a more casual arrangement where there is no formal commitment and where a large degree of independence remains for both parties. There is just an agreement to live together with the details of the arrangement evolving over time.

There are also more radical models being promoted by authors and indeed by individuals who are searching for creative ways to save or change the institution of marriage - or just to spice up their relationships. In some cases, the intention is to ease the pain of divorce by allowing dissolution within an open, pre-determined arrangement. They argue that these new "models" would take away the dishonesty and the shock of separation that now occurs within many marriages. One such arrangement is the "business contract," modeled after corporations that have moved away from hiring "permanent employees" in favor of "contracted personnel" where the responsibilities are detailed within a specified time frame. Similarly, this modern marriage model specifies an "expiry date" or "term limit" that can be extended if the relationship continues to go well.

A second model that appears to be increasingly popular with North Americans might be called the "non-monogamy" arrangement where partners are allowed to have sexual affairs. Some just do it privately and discreetly while others are fully engaged in group, club and party arrangements. "Swinging," also known as wife swapping, or partner swapping, or wife lending, according to one estimate now involves up to 15 million American couples. A number of surveys have reported the vast majority of those couples describe "happy relationships" before swinging, that became "very happy" afterwards. However, these surveys do not include "longitudinal" studies that look at changes in outcome over time.

Opponents of the swinging lifestyle identify moral grounds and health issues as reasons for their disagreement. They also believe that few couples have the personal and relational security to withstand the experience. Over time, jealousy, resentment and emotional connections will place extraordinary stress on the "swinging" couples and the critics predict that the stress will eventually lead to the dissolution of the original partnership. And there is considerable anecdotal evidence to suggest that the critics may be right.

"Wife lending" is not new and can be traced back several hundred years to a number of different cultures in Arabia, Africa, South America and among the Inuit in North America. In more recent years it apparently began in earnest among American military families in the 50's and then spread to the suburbs following the Korean war where many young women were estranged or became widowed after more than 128,000 young American men were killed or wounded.

So today, as millions abandon the traditional marriage arrangement, academics and activists wonder if it is simply an obsolete institution. However, the more traditional and spiritual thinkers who remain proponents of marriage, see the solution to the high divorce rates in terms of addressing the personal and societal reasons that people separate. Abandoning the traditional marriage model, they would argue, is like throwing out the proverbial "baby with the bath water." They contend that the institution has "too much to offer" and can be saved if we honestly address the many causes of divorce and separation.

There we have it, proponents who feel strongly that the institution of marriage is worth fixing and opponents who believe marriage is not, nor will ever again be viable. The institution, they will contend, is obsolete and destined to "go the way of the dinosaur." Proponents say that marriage preserves the family unit and is vital to the maintenance of morals and civilization. They see it as a necessary "legally sanctioned contract" between two people, giving the partners certain rights and obligations.

So where does that leave us in the debate about institutional obsolescence? Is the institution itself no longer relevant in a modern society? Or is the institution needed more than ever in a world that many see as having lost traditional values? Or is the debate simply academic? Whether we believe in the institution or not, marriage is a risky proposition. Whatever one's view of marriage, the real issue is about relationships and not the legal framework. While more and more North Americans think marriage is obsolete and are opting for various cohabitation arrangements, it seems that the debate over the importance of marriage may be somewhat irrelevant, because all forms of family partnerships can fail. And they do. So why focus on the institution of marriage itself? The desire to love, to be loved and to want security seems to have existed forever. Marriage is a human construct, something that came about through the desire of society to regulate human partnerships.

The real question then would seem to be "what is the best way to promote a successful partnership?" Not a marriage necessarily. Given what we know about human nature and the need for connection, security and social relationships, the need for a mutually supportive partnership probably continues to exist. Is your partner sensitive to your wants and feelings? Do they support your goals and aspirations? Are you treated with respect and sensitivity? Do you feel controlled, threatened or manipulated? As a general experience, do you feel close both physically and emotionally?

SECTION 2: *Why them?*

CHAPTER 4: SEARCHING

"Find someone who knows you are not perfect, but treats you as if you are."
                                        The love Bits

Many people believe that the most common location for people in our culture to meet is in a social setting like a restaurant, pub or a bar. The informality and consumption of alcohol can make an introduction - and an exit - easier to manage. But is the energy of a bar really the most conducive to the beginning of a meaningful relationship? One young New Zealand couple advises all of their friends and associates to go to church -where they met. "The church is conducive to starting a relationship the right way," they preach. You may later learn that the church where they met was actually a bar named "The Church." Whether church, bar or some other social setting, statistically they are not the best place to make a meaningful connection. Most people who meet and then develop ongoing relationships do so as Sir Elton John did - through a mutual friend.

"I'm very relaxed. I have a family, I have a partner of 20 years, I have a wonderful life; nothing could be better." Sir Elton John, pianist, singer and composer met his partner David Furnish, a Toronto advertising executive in 1993. They met when a mutual friend invited Furnish to a dinner party at the Elton mansion. David and John met in an environment that friends judged might result in complementary energy and the connection worked. It apparently often does, especially when sensitive and caring people do the enabling.

According to a survey facilitated by Google, more eighteen to thirty-four year olds, some 39 percent met their current significant others through mutual friends. In contrast, some 22 percent said they met "out in a social setting." Interestingly, people who already knew others as "friends" had the highest rate of turning introductions into romantic relationships. Their 40 percent result lapsed the 35 percent of respondents whose relationship started through social introductions or formal dates arranged by acquaintances that were not close friends. Friendship it appears is important, not only at the beginning of a relationship, but throughout it. A Canadian study for example found that spouses who described each other as their "best friends" were happier than those who didn't.

So what about the myriad of Internet dating sites that claim such extraordinary results? Although in one survey 59 percent of Americans said that dating sites were a great place to meet and develop a relationship, less than 10 percent acknowledged that they actually met a "significant other" that way. Social media matches like Facebook have an even lower connection rate at fewer than 6 percent.

When you think about the value of personal connections, the success of relationships evolving from introductions makes a great deal of sense. A mutual friend is trustworthy and people in the same social circles usually share common interests, values and even energy. The new couples then also usually enjoy the ongoing support of friends, an important factor in successful long-term relationships. Personal introductions can also be easier than Internet dating that usually involves flashy photos, intriguing descriptions, a question of honesty of information, a potential expectation of a romance and of course, not really knowing what you are getting.

It was inevitable though that someone would recognize the preference for arranged relationships over cold Internet dating, so there is now an "app" that serves up matches based on mutual "Facebook" friends. Even more "sci-fi" is the controversial "Instant Chemistry" offering where a Canadian company uses DNA research, including a process that they say can determine an individual's "propensity to emotion." The result they claim, is "compatibility matching."

Notwithstanding these new "innovations," recent surveys are consistent with research done several years ago that concluded that the Internet remains the third most likely way of meeting after personal introductions and meeting in drinking establishments. In summary, how people get connected for ongoing romantic relationships has not changed for over a decade with the Internet emerging as a strong contender, with pubs and bars even more popular. However, the most popular and most successful method of meeting that person of your dreams is still an introduction by a personal acquaintance, preferably a friend.

Where did you meet your partner? Did the location matter? Did you judge them to have compatible interests, values and energy? Where would you look if you were to do it over?

CHAPTER 5: PERSONALITY

"I rely on my personality for birth control."
Liz Winston

It seems obvious that the more we know about a potential partner the better equipped we are to understand compatibility and the potential for a long term connection that will work. One of the reasons so many relationships fail is that the choices were all wrong in the first place. Choices often made in a state of "ignorant bliss." The word ignorant means "unaware," "uniformed" and "oblivious" and most people can think back to their marriage decision and will agree that those words were an apt descriptor.

So, how many people could have, or can even today answer the following questions. Did you or do you know what you want from a relationship? Have you had a reasonable number of life experiences and know something about who you are? Do you and your partner have compatible interests and values? Are you rational as well as romantic? Are you fearful that you are getting old or may find no one else? The best way to achieve extensive knowledge about these questions and others is to participate in relationship enrichment courses or psychological counseling, but most people don't go that route. Short of that approach, personality "typing" can be very instructive.

Personality typing theories have been around for a long time and one early form was called the "Four Temperaments," based on work going all the way back to 320 BC and the Greek physician Hippocrates, a man often referred to as the father of modern medicine. The four temperaments theory proposed that there were four fundamental personality types, sanguine (optimistic leader-like), choleric (bad-tempered or irritable), melancholic (analytical and quiet), and phlegmatic (relaxed and peaceful).

A more recent example of personality typing that gained wide public interest was the Type A and Type B theory. The concept was detailed in a 1996 book by American Cardiologist Dr. Marten Friedman and the terms soon became part of everyday conversation, still frequently referred to today. The model describes "Type A" individuals as ambitious, rigidly organized, impatient, status conscious, high-achievers who were prone to heart attacks and who usually smoked tobacco as a way of relieving stress. The theory then described "Type B" individuals as a contrast to "A," generally reflective and living at a lower stress level, working steadily while demonstrating creativity and thoughtfulness.

The Personality Type A and B theories were brought into disrepute when the public learned that the tobacco industry funded the research for decades, pumping millions into studies in an attempt to demonstrate that smoking correlated with a personality type prone to coronary heart disease and cancer. The intended conclusion, prepared for political manipulation, was that the health consequences from smoking were caused by the psychological characteristics of the individual smoker rather than by the tobacco products themselves.

There are however, less controversial and still current personality type theories that can be helpful as tools for self-understanding and self- development. When we refer to a personality "type," we are usually referring to a psychological classification of different groups of individuals. Personality types are different than personality traits, which refer to some tendencies to behave in certain ways. For example, if we talk about types, introverts and extraverts are two fundamentally different categories of people. If we talk about traits, we are referring to introversion and extraversion as existing within one person in varying degrees.

Although some psychologists use models of personality type such as the Enneagram, personality type theories have received considerable criticism from academics and psychometric researchers who believe that it is impossible to explain the diversity of human personalities with a small number of discrete types. Psychological professionals therefore tend to prefer "trait" models such as the so-called "Five factor" classification that analyses human personality in terms of broad categories of behavior:

- Our "openness to new experiences" and "appreciation of life,"
- Our "conscientiousness" and "organization and dependability,"
- Our "extraversion," and our "assertiveness and sociability,"
- Our "agreeableness, compassion and concentration," and finally,
- Our "neuroticism," or ability to handle emotions.

This "Five-factor Model" (FFM) of personality **traits** has been researched many times and has shown remarkable consistency in predicting a number of outcomes including divorce, in different ages and cultures. The model has also been demonstrated to have the ability to be a powerful predictor of an individual's satisfaction with romantic relationships and of personality compatibility. It is one of the least controversial of personality tests and is still used by many psychologists.

The personality **type** models are less popular with professionals because they are considered "unyielding" in that the models imply that an individual would have difficulty living outside of their "types" and the specific predictable behavior the type dictates. For example, if a husband's type were inclined to include a "roving eye," he would inevitably have another relationship. This is of course not necessarily so and anything that predicts behavior with such rigidity is suspect. Whatever one's judgment of the power a "type" might have over an individual, it is generally accepted that typing can provide us with an opportunity to learn more about ourselves and about others.

One of the best known is the "Enneagram of Personality," commonly used in business, relational and spiritual contexts through seminars, conferences, books, magazines, and electronic medium. In the business context it is used to gain insights into workplace dynamics, in personal relations it is used to accelerate the knowledge about and between individuals in new relationships and in a spiritual context it is presented as a path to higher states of being. Developed over generations, the Enneagram of Personality in its current form was originally conceived by a Chilean psychiatrist and brought to the United States in the 1970's. Psychiatrists, psychologists and Jesuit priests once used it extensively, however the criticism of type models in recent years has resulted in lessened use by the scientific community.

The Enneagram of Personality details nine interconnected personality types, with each type having a name that summarizes the person's most prominent traits. In brief, the types are as follows:

- A "Reformer" or rational, idealistic, principled, purposeful, self-controlled and perfectionistic person.
- The "Helper," a caring, demonstrative, generous, people-pleasing, possessive individual.
- The "Achiever," a success-oriented, pragmatic, adaptive, excelling, driven, and image-conscious person.
- The "Individualist," sensitive, withdrawn, expressive, dramatic and temperamental.
- The "Investigator," an intense, perceptive, innovative, secretive and isolated person.
- A "Loyalist," who is committed, security oriented, engaging, responsible, anxious, and suspicious.
- An "Enthusiast" who is busy, fun loving, spontaneous, versatile, distractible and scattered.
- A "Challenger." Powerful, dominating, self-confident, decisive, willful and confrontational, and finally,
- The "Peacemaker," easygoing, self-effacing, receptive, reassuring, agreeable, and complacent.

People don't always fit precisely into any one type and the model identifies additional strong characteristics between types. The Enneagram has many facets to it, one example being compatibility with others and another being the kind of negative and positive behavior that might be expected during high functioning times and through periods of dysfunction. Easily accessible promotional material is available on the Internet including a free "short test."

A fourth personality profiling system known as True Colors has grown in popularity in recent years in part because of its simplicity. The system is described as "a way to understand the behaviors and motivations of others relative to our own personalities." The theory is that everyone's personality contains the colors blue, orange, gold and green with two "dominant" colors representing the core of a person's personality.

- Green personality types are independent thinkers,
- Gold represents pragmatic planners,
- Orange personality types are very action-oriented, and
- Blue personalities are people-oriented.

The belief behind True Colors is that by recognizing personality differences we are able to identify the strengths and challenges in any evolving relationship.

A less scientific and perhaps "tongue in cheek" way of judging the personalities of potential suitors is by observing the cars they drive. Images that may be little more than propaganda by car manufacturers, but nonetheless they might be instructive. A number of market research studies have identified what cars appeal to what type of personality and some people believe those wheels can give clues to age, gender, income level, marital status and even political leanings. But there can be misinterpretations. For example, there are very poor parts of the country such as in ghettos and some Aboriginal/First nation reserves where the only luxury is an automobile.

Even in middle class America the signs can be misleading. For example, the Porsche smacks of success, but the Porsche Boxster that hasn't changed body styles for a decade and is now relatively economical transportation can be easily suggestive of a wealthy driver, and that may or may not be the case. So if we accept the reality that not all drivers of luxury vehicles have money, but that many in mainstream America do, cars can reflect not only assets, but also personality types.

According to surveys, the BMW, Mercedes and Range Rover tend to be driven by people who are admired and who are usually "professional, skilled, ambitious, important, satisfied and comfort-seeking." Even more admired is the important yet conscientious and "Avant-guard" driver of the all-electric Tesla with their desire for speed and class, but sensitivity to silence and the environment. Then there are the rare owners of the UK built Bentley and Rolls Royce automobiles. Quintessentially British, these "understated" vehicles scream wealth and the companies own research confirms that.

The person looking for wealth along with love might find that pursuing the drivers of these cars might pay off in that partnering with these folks could mean money, along with a disappointing realization that the person's personal priorities might be quite independent of working on a relationship. While these luxury beasts have become the ultimate status vehicles, others have found a reputation of more moderate sophistication in owning an Austin Mini, probably due to its British roots and ecological benefits. The owners who are often women convey a message of "sophistication and environmental sensitivity."

At the other end of the continuum in terms of both money and age we find the American coupe. It does however convey the same message about "look at me." The revival of retro cars like the Dodge Charger and Challenger are a testament to the coupes popularity with youth. There are still those "bad boys" who prefer the image of a muscle car or sports convertible, but it might be wise to remember that "bad boys" tend to make for lots of fun, but not necessarily within a long term relationship.

The "pick-up" truck is increasingly popular and some northern automobile dealerships seem to sell little else. No longer just utilitarian, the trucks are equipped with luxurious interiors and stylish bodies and they work hard to convey that they belong to practical, no-nonsense, strong, hard-working folk. Perhaps those are the same characteristics of a great mate?

Then there is the minivan, that favorite of families. It conveys, practicality, family values, enthusiasm about sports and little concern with image. The minivans suburban neighbor the "SUV" conveys similar values, but with the added message of more status and the power to go anywhere anytime. The station wagon, family sedan, crossover and mid-size all convey a similar message of middle class urban America, perhaps unsure of just what to buy and some would say overly concerned with the economy, environment, mileage, reliability and cup-holders. The economy vehicles like the Honda Civic have drivers that are usually frugal, practical and generally unconcerned with image, while sedan owners like the Chevrolet Impala are viewed as more "Heartland America" than most - conservative, staid and probably a Republican or Conservative voter.

If we recognize the limitations of generalizing, whether that is related to vehicles, types or traits, personality assessment can be a valuable aid when used as a tool for self- understanding, or for a better understanding of those we want to know better. An assessment can provide important information on their values, interests, likes and dislikes, insights that might otherwise take considerable time to develop. And they are insights that can be vital. For example, an individual with a high value in following rules may have difficulty with a person who likes to "live on the edge." A partier may have difficulty with a quiet, introspective person and vice versa. An "odd couple," one of which is neat, tidy and sanitary will invariably have difficulty with a partner who is slovenly. The list of problematic differences in values, interests, likes and dislikes can be very lengthy and unfortunately many of them often don't "rear their ugly head" until well into a relationship.

There are social scientists that believe personality is a major factor in the choice of a partner and that we tend to look for someone who is similar to ourselves. Others believe we find a partner who is similar to a parent or parents. Yet others believe we choose partners who are different from ourselves. This view is not necessarily taken from the perspective that opposites attract, but on the principle that people with different personalities provide different and complimentary skills in dealing with the world, but still have common interests. Other researchers have espoused a view that there are many factors that have an influence on marriage choices and while personality may be taken into account, there is no overall pattern to personality attraction.

Notwithstanding these views, the "Big Five Factor Markers" of personality traits has been shown to be very predictive of outcomes in marriage. While the best information can be derived from this process by a trained psychologist, it is possible to use the model for educational or self-interest purposes. The results however should not be interpreted as any kind of diagnosis or psychological advice, but rather as information about oneself or one's mate; a tool for greater insight and consciousness. The technique asks a number of questions in order to "summarize an individual" and the test can be found free of charge at *personality-testing.info/BIGS.php* The analysis consists of fifty statements where you will be asked to select the most appropriate response on a five-point scale. It takes about ten minutes to complete and at the end of the assessment you will be asked if your responses can be anonymously kept and used for research. You are free to decline.

Two other systems that can provide considerable information on a prospective mate are also available on line. The Enneagram and True Colors are personality "type" instruments and as such carry with them the limitations of possible over-generalization. The Enneagram "short" or "sample" test or True Colors quiz can be used in a private environment or even at a social such as a dinner party - if the participants understand the nature of the quiz and the requirement for self-disclosure. The Enneagram test, which consists of 36 questions, each requiring a forced choice of one of two options is free and can be found at *9types.com* It takes about 10 minutes to complete. A longer more detailed evaluation is available for a fee. The True Colors test also uses multiple-choice questions and at the completion a detailed forty-page report is prepared for you. The test can be taken on-line at *truecolorsintl.com* but there is a charge for this one. The entire process can prove to be very instructive. The participants can learn in one evening, more about a potential partner and relationship than they might otherwise learn over months and years.

Did you understand your own personality characteristics when you met your partner? Did you understand theirs? Are you and your partner similar? Is your partner similar to one of your parents? Is your partner similar to one or both of their parents and do you perceive that as good, bad or irrelevant? Is your partner quite different from you? Are your interests different? Are your character traits complimentary? Have either of you changed dramatically over time? Do you still enjoy your partner's personality "type?"

CHAPTER 6: HOMOSEXUALITY

"Like me, the great majority of Americans wish both to preserve the traditional definition of marriage and to oppose bias and intolerance directed towards gays and lesbians."

Mitt Romney

The quote by Mr. Romney could be a joke, but unfortunately it is not. The 2012 Republican candidate for President, Mitt Romney exposed himself as a stereotypical politician attempting to please both sides in a controversy. A controversy that has destroyed many lives over many decades. A controversy stemming from attitudes of prejudice, discrimination, rejection and shame in homes and communities across North America. Attitudes that have resulted in unconscious denial, conscious renunciation and public secrecy regarding peoples own sexuality.

Then through insight or perhaps fueled by greater tolerance or public indifference, thousands who have engaged in heterosexual relationships and often born children, have in contemporary terms "come out of the closet" and acknowledged their own sexuality. A situation that is all too frequently devastating for a partner who view the situation as a personal rejection rather than their partners own acceptance of their real self. The response is inevitably one of repulsion, anger, shame and rejection. For the individual entering a new homosexual relationship, they often wade into deep uncharted waters.

Despite the fact that history tells us that humans have never limited their sexual pleasure to what we now call heterosexual intercourse, the history of "homosexuality" or "gay" relationships as we now know it, is relatively short. (In recent years the acronym LGBT (lesbian, gay, bisexual and transgender) has increasingly replaced the gay term with even more recent use of LGBTIQ (adding "intersex" and "queer.")

Looking back to the mid 1800's in Europe, the governments began noticing that people were moving off of the farms and into the cities away from their parishes, families and away from arranged marriages where the parents determined their offspring's partners. The officials viewed these relationships as dangerous for the parishes and described them as "sexually deviant," with one such class called "homosexuals."

Prejudice towards "homosexuality" grew from this period and historical records detail where people organized in support of each other as early as the late 1800's. Although they quickly became the target of significant discrimination, both informally and officially, the groups continued to grow through the early 1900's. Their progress was then virtually halted during the 1930's and 40's when thousands of homosexual people were sent to die in concentration camps in and around Nazi Germany. And the rest of the world seemed unsympathetic.

Life can be difficult. Life as a "homosexual" can be even more difficult. Relationships are challenging. Homosexual relationships can be even more challenging. Ending an intimate relationship is usually difficult. Ending a "gay" relationship can be even more so. Like their heterosexual counterparts, gay couples separate for many reasons, but they also have added stresses. They are likely to experience social and cultural pressures and they are also more likely to be two-income families with no children - which in the straight population have a higher risk of divorce.

Couples who get into legal relationships like marriage rarely think in advance as to how to get out, and so it is with gay couples. But their problems can be much greater than for the heterosexual duo. For example, court processes are more complex and therefore legal costs are higher. Even finding a knowledgeable and sympathetic lawyer can be difficult. Where children are involved, one or both of the parents may not be the biological parent and if they failed to ensure a legal adoption their lawful standing might be affected. Same-sex couples splitting property or assets may also face a government gift tax that doesn't apply to straight couples.

The couples in same-sex marriages can generally only obtain a divorce in jurisdictions that recognize same-sex marriages. For example, a couple that was legally married in Massachusetts and then moved to Florida or Texas would be unable to divorce. In 2004 Canada became the first country in the world to legislate the granting of divorces to same-sex couples. Perhaps not surprising for Canada, because the country was also early to recognize same-sex marriages. Hundreds of gay and lesbian couples from around the world travelled to Canada in order to celebrate their relationships with a legal marriage ceremony. But at the time, no one gave a moment's thought to the possibility that these marriages, like that of their heterosexual counterparts, might fragment into divorce in the future.

Canada's Divorce Act, which had not initially considered the influx of marriages involving non-resident visitors, required that one of the spouses reside in Canada for one year prior to the granting of a divorce, a condition that was of course very difficult for a non-resident to comply with. In 2013 an amendment to the Marriage Act permitted a same-sex couple to apply for a divorce in the jurisdiction where they married, without a residency requirement, even if they lived in an American state that did not permit same-sex marriage. Additionally, each of the spouses would have to consent to the granting of a divorce, unless circumstances prevented such consent and then a Court order waiving consent was required, either

49

from a Canadian court, or a Court where the couple resided during their marriage.

In the U.S. and Canada, the history of the so called "third" sexual culture and politics has been much shorter than in Europe and Asia and ironically was largely driven by the military establishment where many young men lived in the same settings such as "barracks." Then came the ban on gays in the military where thousands of gay and lesbian people were dishonorably discharged from the armed services and dumped in port cities. As an example, several hundred ex-service people were for a period deposited in San Francisco each day. Unwilling to go home in disgrace, they stayed. Other enclaves grew in New York, Los Angeles and Vancouver.

In both Europe and North America, public disclosure of homosexuality was enough to get people fired from their jobs, ostracized from families and communities and brutalized by police. Many committed suicide. Even notable heroes like Britain's Alan Turing whose innovative computer technology broke Nazi codes resulting in critically important British naval victories, was not exempt from discrimination. Turing was prosecuted in 1952 for homosexual acts and he accepted a form of chemical castration by psychiatrists in order to avoid prison. He committed suicide in 1954.

Under U. S. President Dwight Eisenhower, a former military General himself, homosexuality became by executive order a sufficient reason to fire any federal employee from their job. Many companies followed suit. The FBI under J. Edgar Hoover, himself a "closet gay," hunted out and harmed homosexuals. Over the subsequent decades the "gay and lesbian" movements grew in spite of the discrimination and in response to the aggression, become more militant themselves with public protests and even rioting occurring in several large U.S. cities. Attitudes then seemed to begin to shift, albeit slowly and with those changes came political leadership.

One notable leader Pierre Trudeau, father of the 2015 Canadian Prime Minister Justin Trudeau, was in 1967 the Canadian Justice Minister and would later become Prime Minister. He proposed major changes to Canada's criminal code including the de-criminalization of homosexuality. In a now famous speech in support of the proposed legislation he said, "Take this thing on homosexuality, I think the view we take here is that there's no place for the state in the bedrooms of the nation. I think that what's done in private between adults doesn't concern the Criminal Code."

The New Democratic Party leader Tommy Douglas speaking in support of the bill said, "If ever we needed in this country to adopt a new attitude towards homosexuality, this is the time. Instead of treating it as a crime, and driving it underground, we ought to recognize it for what it is; it's a mental illness, it's a psychiatric condition which ought to be treated sympathetically by psychiatrists and social workers. We're not going to do this by tossing people into jail." The law went into effect in 1969, setting in place a Canadian societal view that homosexuals were not to be seen as bad, only as mad.

Human rights advocates rejected the view that homosexuality was an illness, however the passage of the Canadian law helped to buoy U.S. activists and through the early 1970's gay and lesbian communities pushed for de-criminalization and anti-discrimination laws in several major cities and within professional organizations across the U.S. In December of 1973 the movements achieved what they described as a "major victory" by convincing the American Psychiatric Association (APA) to "remove homosexuality from its list of mental illnesses."

In reality, the way psychiatrists were already looking at homosexuality had changed from viewing it as a treatable condition to that of only treating the distress related to the condition. The official view of the APA really hasn't changed in the past forty years and in 2013 the Diagnostic & Statistical Manual 5 for Mental Disorders described the disorder not in terms of the orientation itself, but in the context of "a strong and persistent cross gender identification" and "persistent discomfort about one's assigned sex or a sense of the appropriateness in the gender role of that sex."

In the forty years between 1973 and 2013, the view of professionals within the behavioral and social sciences community was increasingly that homosexuality is simply a variation of human sexual orientation. The American Psychological Association followed the Psychiatric Associations lead and eventually the World Health Organization supported the growing consensus that same-sex sexual and romantic attractions, feelings, and behaviors are "healthy variations" of human sexuality, although some therapists still maintain that it is a disorder.

American lawmakers were far behind the scientists in terms of attitude and as late as 1986 the U.S. Supreme Court held that states had a right to criminalize consensual homosexual behavior, even when the act was committed in private. The gay community was incensed and the following year, one of the largest civil rights demonstrations in the country's history drew more than 650,000 people to Washington D.C. Those demonstrations grew in numbers and frequency over the next thirty years, yet homosexual people continued to battle against "bias and intolerance" as former presidential candidate Mitt Romney put it.

That bias and intolerance is probably not greater in any place than it is in regard to the legal union of gay couples. In 2005 Canada became the third country in the world and the first outside of Europe to pass a law enabling gay people to marry. It took litigation and a Supreme Court decision, but the Liberal government under Liberal Prime Minister Jean Chretien provided for marriage and full benefits to same sex couples. Then a year later when Conservative Prime Minister Stephen Harper was elected he attempted to have the matter reconsidered and reversed by the legislators, but he had only a minority government and was unsuccessful in his attempt.

In the United States opposition to same sex marriages was more strident and in 1996 the Federal government passed an Act that said no state needed to recognize the validity of the marriages. Most of the opposition to gay marriages had come from states like Alabama and Arkansas in the Deep South, along with the support of the more fundamental religions there and in the state of Utah. During that period a number of Americans travelled and even moved to Canada in order to marry.

Then in 2010 a Massachusetts Judge agreed that the Federal governments denial of rights and benefits to marriages was unconstitutional and required that governments provide benefits. The action that followed was essentially recognition of the non-traditional marriage by the U.S. government and that decision eventually led to the legalization of same sex unions by most states. Seventy percent of Americans were able to get marriage licenses by 2015.

Ironically, after decades of fighting for the acceptance of same-sex marriages, many couples found themselves searching for ways to divorce. In the United States in 2011, States with available data reported that the marriage dissolution rates for same-sex couples was almost half of the divorce rate for same-sex couples. In contrast some studies reported the rate as higher, also noting that female lesbian divorce was twice the rate of male gay divorce.

The countries of Norway and Sweden have the longest history of same-sex marriages and their leaders originally thought that when people waited years for a chance to marry they might be expected to have a higher than usual level of commitment and stability. Yet some gay and lesbian couples divorced just months after they married.

In summary, couples considering a same-sex marriage or common-law relationship need to carefully contemplate if a legal marriage is in fact in their best interest. If they choose marriage, they need to know the laws and processes with respect to both marriage and divorce for the jurisdiction in which they live. And the laws throughout America remain tenuous under President Trump who has openly criticized the June 2015 Supreme Court decision which decreed that the American constitution guarantees a right to same-sex marriage. At that time Justice Anthony M. Kennedy of the U.S. Supreme Court wrote for the majority opinion: "No longer may this liberty be denied." The Supreme Courts attitude could change after the 2018 Trump nomination of the Honorable Brett Kavanagh. While Canadian laws regarding lesbian, gay, bisexual and transgender relationships are well defined and national in scope, in the U.S. marriage and divorce are complex and vary by jurisdiction and continue to change as a result of U.S. Supreme Court decisions.

Notwithstanding modern liberal legal thinking, it would be naive for gay couples not to expect they will still need to deal with prejudice and discrimination. Times and attitudes have most certainly changed since British war hero Alan Turing was charged with homosexual behavior in 1952 and some evidence of that fact can be found in the general public and media response to the Supreme Court's 2015 decision, along with the attention and accolades bestowed on American Olympic hero Bruce Jenner. Early in the same month as the Court's decision, Jenner was featured on the cover of "Vanity Fair" magazine. Appearing as Caitlyn Jenner, the American folk hero once described as the "world's greatest athlete," seemed to receive universal media acclaim after years of trans-gender work, including a reported ten-hour facial "feminization surgery." Jenner's "Twitter" account grew faster than any other over history, including that of American President Barack Obama after his election.

Although polls currently show that 90 percent of Americans say they "know and accept" someone who is lesbian, gay, bisexual or transgender, prejudice and discrimination towards homosexual individuals remains very much alive in the villages and cities across North America. Public attitudes towards homosexuality began to really shift in the late 1990's. A 1991 survey reported that 72 percent of Americans thought homosexual behavior was "always wrong," while a repeat of that survey in 2010 concluded that 44 percent of Americans thought that homosexual behavior was "always wrong." The 2013 "Global Attitudes" study concluded that 71 to 80 percent of North Americans believe homosexuals should be "accepted by society," representing a dramatic shift in attitudes. The 2018 election of openly gay Jared Polis as Governor of Colorado may well provide some evidence of that shift. While laws, official sanctions and media attitudes have changed, the subtler, covert and passive-aggressive attitudes of some members of the population in both Canada and the U.S. continue to be hurtful.

There are some questions you may wish to ask yourself when contemplating the subject "stay or go." Can you remain in a relationship with differing sexual orientations? Are you legally married? Did you wed in a jurisdiction that allows both marriage and divorce? Do you have a pre-nuptial agreement to address custody and property matters? If you adopted, have any non-biological partner or partners completed a legal adoption? Do you understand local laws regarding child custody, asset division and income tax? Do you have a knowledgeable lawyer? (Organizations like the "Lambda Legal" and the "National Center for Lesbian Rights" in the U.S. can help.) Do you have a support system of individuals who understand and accept you?

CHAPTER 7: HEREDITY

"Your genetics load the gun. Your lifestyle pulls the trigger."

Dr. Mehmet Oz

There are very few adults that want to follow in their parents' footsteps, but they do. Children from separated parents for example, are twice as likely to separate themselves. As they age, it is common for people to express the thought (fear) that they are becoming like their parents. Ironically most men and women will also remember the dream of wanting to be like their parents; the dream that sometimes later became a nightmare. Why is that so? Perhaps it is a natural thing, part of the evolution of "man-kind." Most of us want to do and be better than our parents and greater knowledge and consciousness should allow us to do and be just that.

There are no perfect parents, nor have there ever been. The parenting approaches of the past are not as a rule generally better than those used today. Most approaches were probably worse. There are those who would disagree as in "spare the rod and spoil the child," but the evidence is pretty clear that the corporal punishment approach (discipline is a different matter) simply breeds angry people.

While it is wise to learn from the past, in this striving for improvement, many people are inclined to want to reject earlier approaches and with that, much of what their parents were. Beyond wanting to change the way their parents behaved, many people even feel discomfort when they see certain mannerisms or hear familiar words and phrases that they utter. Or they look in a mirror and catch a glimpse of someone recognizable and it isn't just them. And the older they get the more conspicuous the experience becomes.

Adolescents frequently like to believe that they will not be like their parents, but for most, they are simply living in denial. If you are in a relationship, have a look at your partner and then have a look at their parents. Which parent do they seem most like? You can probably now imagine what your partner will look like and perhaps behave like, in 20 to 30 years. Why is that? There are at least three reasons. The first is genetics. Modern neuroscience is only beginning to uncover some of the secrets of our make-up. We are inheriting far more than the color of our skin and eyes. It is now evident that some of the conditions that we have historically blamed on our environment actually have a genetic base. There are many examples, from our pre-disposition to certain disorders like cancer and heart conditions to psychological disorders like some depressive illnesses, schizophrenia, bipolar disorder, anorexia and addiction.

There are those who believe that it is possible that human traits such as extraordinary skills in music and even memory that are sometimes attributed to "past life" experiences, may actually be genetically transferred from ancestors. Every generation has more knowledge and skill than the last and it doesn't just come from education. The brains in each generation seem to be changing, just witness the seemingly natural computer skills in today's children.

In many cases a condition may not be inherited so much as there is a predisposition to certain circumstances. Some research has suggested that there may even be built in tendencies as to how we act. While genes for traits like eye color and height are easy to understand, genes for behavior raise a whole new dimension. They beg the question, are we really responsible for our decisions or couldn't we help ourselves because of our genes? We do know that genes cause some behaviors in animals, for example a border collie will instinctively herd sheep and a Dachshund will burrow without being taught. Similarly, some simple human behaviors are inborn, such as the startle and sucking reflexes of a baby.

So is it possible that a decision as complicated as leaving a relationship is determined by our genes? In search of these answers, scientists compared identical twins that have a matching genetic make-up with those of fraternal twins, whose genome is akin to that of any other brother or sister. One such study attempted to figure out if genes might influence marriage and divorce. The researchers found that there was no difference when it came to getting married, but if one twin in an identical twin pair divorced, the other twin was much more likely to get divorced than was the case with fraternal twins. Their study conclusion was that genetics played some role in divorce.

Another aspect of recent findings in neuroscience relates to our cellular development. Through our environmental experiences we develop "neural pathways" where behaviors are essentially "hard-wired" into our brains. Our early programming in those young developmental years is very powerful and in computer language, it becomes our brains "default" program.

The third reason we are like our parents is because they are the major behavioral influences for most of us through a good portion of our lives. Their beliefs and attitudes were absorbed as we spent our childhood watching them, soaking in how they thought, how they behaved and how they did things. Of course, we also witnessed their views towards themselves and others. Once again our computer-like brains become programmed to that default setting and unless we change those settings, we will probably revert to the familiar path set during those early years.

Recent research may have also found a fourth reason we may be like our parents and how that may contribute to a happy or disruptive relationship. Investigators in the human genome project have found a gene involved in the regulation of serotonin that in turn determines just how important emotions are for different people. All humans inherit a copy of a gene variant called an "allele" from each parent. In the studies, those with two short alleles were bothered by emotion in relationships while those with one or two long alleles were much less bothered by the emotional tenor of their relationship, whether positive or negative. The conclusion was that a relationship between two people with intense emotional levels could be a predictor of a highly volatile experience.

Whether we like it or not, the reality is that our parents have a huge influence on who we are. And it is here that life gets even more complicated. Not only are we likely to become like our parents, but we also subconsciously search for people like them. In summary, not only do they influence who we are, they influence whom we select in a mate. Our earliest relationships with our parents and particularly with our mother, have a lasting influence on our connections in later life, both platonic and romantic. It is quite likely that we begin to form ideas of the ideal partner over the first four to six years of life. As a young child we carry an unconscious mental list of the qualities we want in a partner. We even develop early preferences for body type and as we reach puberty the radar begins to actively search for that model.

The quality of our upbringing will also influence who we look for. Secure children with loving parents tend to have secure, close and loving adult relationships. Children raised in a home where insecurity is felt, tend to have a negative view of themselves and they look to others for validation. They can be needy and demanding in relationships and will move from one partner to another, often the same relationship with a different body. Children from homes where the parent or parents were neglectful or openly hostile tend to be distrustful and independent and will frequently have a difficult time developing close relationships. It is believed that all of these children will be drawn on an unconscious level towards what is familiar to them, good and bad.

In addition to our subconscious search for partners who seem familiar, it is also possible that we look to marry people like our parents for deeper psychological reasons. We might for example choose a partner with a similar personality to a parent in an effort to resolve a troublesome issue that caused us distress as a child, kind of a desperate late effort to get the love and attention we longed for.

So assuming we are pre-ordained to be much like our parents, what does or did this all mean in terms of our choice of partners, the kind of relationships we have and our potential for separation? To begin, we need to understand how they specifically influenced us and how that has affected who we are as unique individuals today.

While it is normal to sound and act like our parents, no matter how hard we try to be different, it doesn't mean we have to become them. The key to changing anything is to understand the problem at its root and then to make a conscious and concerted effort to change it. Otherwise, we are probably doomed to repeating history. We may not have liked a parent or parent's attitudes and behaviors, but if we can look with understanding and insight at their life within the world they experienced, we might discover that from an adult's point of view, what they did wasn't all bad or all wrong. We can try to understand "why" they did certain things the way they did. Some behaviors may be hard to accept, but most of us do the best we can with the knowledge and resources that we have.

Do you believe your parents made the decisions they did from the level of knowledge, emotional maturity and life experience that they had at the time? Can you forgive them for any failures and move-on? Do you understand that those family experiences influence why you make the choices that you do? Are you able to cherish, honor and maintain your relationship with your family of origin, but recognize that as an adult you need to develop a sense of independence and autonomy, making the psychological shift from boy to man or girl to woman? What does this say to you about your "stay or go" question?

CHAPTER 8: ENERGY

"Energy cannot be created or destroyed, it can only be changed from one form to another."
                                        Albert Einstein

Most of us were taught in science class that we are composed of matter. Science is now telling us that the entire universe including each of us, are at our core, raw energy. This new science, often referred to as "quantum physics," has huge implications for people and their relationships because it means we must learn to be aware of the different environments we are in and whether we are getting entangled in destructive or constructive energy waves. Most humans unfortunately have never conditioned themselves to attend to feelings or energy. We have certainly not considered the energy in our words, but rather just respond to the literal meaning of verbal messages.

On the other hand, there are more than a few people who are very conscious about energy transfer and even report receiving messages over very long distances; like receiving a radio wave from the hundreds around us. However, in order to receive a specific radio station we need to tune it in, which is also the case for receiving energy messages from others. But more and more people are now tuning in. In the year 2006 authors Esther and Jerry Hicks published a book entitled *"The Power of Attraction"* that built on their 2004 publication, *"Ask And It Is Given."* Each of these publications - and numerous others since - all contain a common theme that "what we think we become." Our thoughts are raw energy, they said, and they "work like a magnet." If those energy vibrations have expanding, uplifting, spiritual qualities we will draw those qualities to us. Other vibrations, such as those based on fear, anger, victimization or lack, will attract the same qualities, including the people who exhibit those qualities.

Have you ever wondered why people attract the same people over and over? Have you ever wondered why people gravitate to certain people in a group? Have you ever noticed that a person with an addiction can identify a person with similar problems without saying a word? All of us have been with people who leave us feeling happy and energized, while others leave us feeling completely drained. Most of us have also walked into a room where there are arguments and so much tension that it could "be cut with a knife." We are of course feeling negative energy. We are experiencing electro-magnetic fields.

The science of quantum physics declares that our body is atomic in structure and at the center of each atom there is nothing but energy waves. We are a kind of a miniature tornado that generates electricity. All of these atoms are continuously generating trillions of volts of light and heat, and not surprisingly, the theory goes that this energy becomes entangled in the energy of others. These "electro-magnetic" energy fields can be measured by scientists and can be felt by some individuals who are more sensitive to their existence.

The Chinese call this energy "chi" and many individuals have been sensitive to its effect for generations. In fact, most Eastern cultures have used this knowledge in their relationships, treatments and spirituality. In the West we have tended to see the body as a machine comprised of parts and functions - anatomy and physiology. In the East the body is seen as an open energy system with the ability to change. In the West the brain is a computer, while in the East it is believed there is a mind and soul connection that powers the brain.

Imagine all of this energy being generated and then transmitted by us, with each atom vibrating at a different speed. Those vibrations become entwined with those of other people and depending on the inter-relationship of those vibrations, the result can be positive or negative. Some of this we seem to know intuitively, for example we have heard for years the terms "they have positive vibes," or "they have negative vibes."

Unfortunately, most people stumble through life without consciously evaluating or sometimes even being aware of the energy transfer to and from those around them. They might take a lesson from our canine friends who appear to be particularly adept at picking up these waves and then responding to whether the energy is good for them or not.

As early as 1932 American author Emmett Fox wrote, "People are beginning to understand today something of the power of thought to shape the individual's destiny - they know vaguely that thoughts are things - but how the great Law of thought is to be applied they do not know." Seventy-two years later, public interest in the power of energy and thought grew dramatically following the release of the 2004 documentary movie *"What The Bleep Do We Know"* and then in 2006 by the movie and best-selling book *"The Secret"* by Rhonda Byrnes. With over 21 million copies in print, the books tenant is that the universe is governed by a "law" that works like a large magnet and attracts into a person's life the people and events that match their thoughts and feelings - the energy that they emanate.

Some scientists now believe that even our words contain energy. In an admittedly controversial attempt to try and prove the relationship between energy and words, Dr. Masaru Emoto, a Japanese scientist, photographed frozen water crystals after he attached both positive and negative phrases to bottles of water that he had placed in the cold over-night. In that study, the positive and negative messages affected the water differently. When photographed microscopically, positive thoughts created brilliant intricate designs while negative thoughts produced irregular disjointed patterns. One conclusion of that research was that our thinking affects the molecular structure of water, and if that is so, then surely our thoughts affect human cells that in adults contain an average of 55 to 65 percent water.

So if these theories are correct and we attract to our life, experiences that match our energy vibrations, that we attract whatever we give our attention and energy to, that we attract both who we are and what we expect, then it will be true that, "what we think about, we can bring about." So if we wish have a relationship devoid of extreme dysfunction, or if we want to avoid attracting the same people over and over again, or we wish to find the partner of our dreams, it may well be possible by simply changing our thinking.

So how do we change our thinking? Much of who we are is learned in the first four to six years of life and how we think is part of that learning. How then do we possibly change that thinking? The answer is that some of that learning needs to be "unlearned." Medical science now tells us that once our behaviors become habits - repeated patterns of behavior that over time become automatic and then tend to occur subconsciously - they become "hard wired" into our brains and then are difficult to change. Kind of like the old adage "you can't teach an old dog new tricks." And although it may be true that our thinking becomes hard-wired, it is still possible to change.

When we repeatedly respond to a brain message in the same way, whether it is a positive or negative message, we teach the brain to respond in that way the next time. For example, if we respond to those we don't like with hostility and aggression, perhaps associated with a drink of alcohol, then over time, on every occasion that we feel challenged, our brain will link alcohol, anger and aggression. Essentially our brains neurons become programmed for that response and the reaction comes automatically and unconsciously. This fight mechanism is then considered by the brain to be necessary for survival and it becomes a habit. Every time we respond to a challenge in that manner our brain circuits become stronger and more difficult to change, but not impossible.

It is rather like breaking a new trail in a heavily wooded forest. Over time the vegetation is shoved aside and the earth becomes trampled and packed. The terrain will become easier and easier to traverse and walking through an area that might have once been an effort, becomes routine and easy. If the trail becomes blocked, say by a fallen tree and a new trail is forged, it will again take conscious effort and time in order to build a new path that works with the ease of the previous one.

This change in one's thought process will over time become a habit, resulting in a new neural pathway in the brain that will affect the physiology of the brain and ultimately every organ and gland (the body). This process in medical terms is called "neuroplasticity," that in its simplest terms, means that the brain develops, but can also change its structure and composition in response to changes in its environment. Parts of the brain, including its circuitry take on new roles and functions. In other words, it is possible to reprogram the brain to think the thoughts that we want and that will produce the energy that will serve us best.

In order to reprogram our brain, we must begin with setting an "intention." The challenge with doing so is largely contained in what we believe. If we don't believe something will work, it usually won't. For example, if someone throws a ball at us and we believe we cannot catch it, we probably won't. So when we encounter doubt, we know we have gone beyond our range of belief and we need to alter our thinking.

The theory also suggests that in order to attract more of what we want in life we must be grateful for what we have, because gratitude provides the mental avenue to focus our energy on more of what we truly love. Tracking what we value also provides a reminder and evidence of all of the "good" that we do have. And even the circumstances we judge to be "bad" can have value because we can learn from those experiences. Indeed, many times, what appears to be a negative experience turns out to be a positive one when we look back at it over time. This is sometimes the case after a difficult divorce or separation.

The theory of energy transfer essentially means that whatever the conscious mind thinks and believes, the subconscious mind will begin to create. Unfortunately, some people create the things they don't want in their life, but this pattern of manifesting can be shifted and reprogrammed through conscious thought and focus. Through this work, people sometimes experience and report almost instantaneous manifestations, while at other times the wait can be lengthy. Either way, they can and usually do facilitate a desired outcome.

The theory in summary, is that in order to expedite a manifestation of our desires - to get what we want - we must first be very clear about the desired outcome. We must then give that desire some energy through repeated thought, including the belief that the outcome is possible. Belief is energy, so if there is no confidence in the outcome, it is unlikely to be realized. Finally, we need to take some action towards achieving the outcome.

Do you work at being sensitive to the energy around you? Do you focus your thinking on energy vibrations that have positive, optimistic, grateful, spiritual qualities? Do you trust your intuition and leave experiences and situations that don't feel right, staying where the energy is good? How would you judge the energy in your current relationship?

CHAPTER 9: CONSCIOUSNESS

"No problem can be solved from the same level of consciousness that created it."
Albert Einstein

While research tells us that communication, money and infidelity are the big drivers of divorce, it is quite possible that consciousness is the big driver of successful relationships. If we accept that the human body is indeed an energy field and that we vibrate at frequencies that will attract the same frequencies, then in the context of relationships, we will attract the people who will exhibit and return our qualities. It is therefore an important part of our consideration of whether to stay or go, that we develop sensitivity to, and insight about, what we are thinking, what we are feeling, who we are and how we affect others. In other words, consciousness.

To be conscious is much more than just being awake. Canadian psychiatrist Richard Bucke author of "Cosmic Consciousness" distinguished between three types of consciousness: *Simple Consciousness*, an awareness of the body, possessed by many animals; *Self Consciousness*, an awareness of being aware, possessed only by humans; and *Cosmic Consciousness*, awareness of the life and order of the universe, possessed only by humans who he described as "enlightened." Many people think that the "enlightened" were only religious leaders, people like Jesus, Siddhartha Gautama, the Dalai Lama, Mohammed and Ernest Holmes, or they were scientific and political leaders like Socrates, Albert Einstein, Mahatma Gandhi, Nelson Mandela, Martin Luther-King and Abraham Lincoln.

But look around, there are many many more. People at a younger and younger age are becoming more interested in self-exploration. For many, a sense of purpose is becoming more important than money and career. There appears to be less interest in blaming others for one's position in life and more interest in taking personal responsibility. Many young people seem to be getting a clearer understanding of the importance of their thoughts, feelings and experiences and are striving to be the kind of person they truly value, rather than trying to change the people around them.

So how do we evolve to a greater consciousness as to thoughts, feelings, who we are and how we affect others? How do we manage our thinking? How do we become more enlightened? All of the world's religious leaders who were considered enlightened, reported achieving that sense of inner knowledge and peace through what they described as "stillness." There are records dating some four thousand years ago that detailed the efforts of Yogic masters in India to develop methods to deepen their consciousness. Two thousand years ago a man named Patanjali consolidated the teachings and wrote detailed instructions on how to achieve stillness in documents he named the "Yoga Sutras." Central to Patanjalis work was an awareness of breathing. The Hindu term "prana," means breath and it has been a central part of that religions development throughout history.

About the same time that the Yogic masters were developing their theories, the Taoist meditation traditions were being developed in China. A man by the name of Lao Tzu is recorded at the center of this teaching and his text the Tao Te Ching is one of the most extensively read spiritual texts of all time. The Taoist goal was to quiet the flow of thoughts that race through the mind in order to expose the deeper more meaningful beliefs. The Buddha, whose real name was Siddhartha Gautama, was born about a century after Patanjali and Lao Tzu. His central meditative teaching was that we needed to get in touch with the present moment. His views were consistent with the writing of most contemporary "new thought" authors like Eckhart Tolle who believe that most of our fears are "psychological," come from looking at the past and future and that we need to try and stay rooted in the present.

Four hundred years after Buddha, Jesus taught that love was the center of spiritual life and that in order to love, we needed to accept life as it is today, while working towards improvement. Jesus taught that peace of mind and inner quiet were essential to experiencing that change. About five centuries after Christ, Mohammed taught the Islamic culture that he saw humans as harmonious and good. The root of the word Islam is the word peace and Mohammed taught that surrendering to Allah was best done through meditation.

In essence, each spiritual leader's instructions, whether Patanjali, Lao Tzu, the Buddha, Jesus or Mohammed, all were similar. As a result, every major religion has over time encouraged stillness as a way of reaching the individual's center or core of being. Consistent with these spiritual teachings, enlightened leaders like Socrates, Einstein, Gandhi, Mandela, Luther-King and Lincoln have all encouraged stillness as way to self-knowledge. A place where they were able to realize a deeper wisdom, purpose and vitality. A place where they better understood who they were and how their feelings, thoughts and actions affected others.

The reason for stillness of course, is to quiet the mind so that we are better able to be aware of our conscious thoughts. One of the most common ways to stillness is through meditation, a strategy relatively new to North American, but the numbers who understand it and now use it are growing rapidly. One study reported its use by over ten percent of North American adults. In addition to religions, the approach is being adopted by educators for relaxation, concentration and creativity, by business for improved productivity and job satisfaction and by many medical, psychological and psychotherapy practices for stress reduction, pain relief and even for disease treatment through cellular renewal and re-generation.

The mind is always working, with over 50 thoughts, sensations and impulses recorded every minute. That's almost 60,000 per day. The mind is also continuously creating and what it constructs will depend upon our thoughts and feelings at any given point in time. It is here that the process of managing our thinking becomes quite difficult. In the first instance, much of what goes on within those thousands of thoughts is unconscious and so by definition we are not even aware of them.

Almost anything can bubble up from the subconscious. We are of course not responsible for the ideas that emerge, but we are responsible for what we do with those ideas after they arise. This knowledge would have probably been helpful for the young Catholic children who were told an early age that bad thoughts were sins. As the ideas popped into their heads they tried to purge themselves of them so that they didn't have to prepare a lengthy confessional list. If they had realized that they were only responsible for what they did with those ideas, they might not have needed that confessional at all. Well perhaps occasionally.

The decisions we make in our conscious mind about the uncontrollable flood we receive from the unconscious mind are all that we should reasonably be considered responsible for. It is what we call "free-will," or in some cases "free-won't," responses that sometimes require controlling, or at least corralling. We can tell ourselves that we are going to remain calm all day and then someone cuts us off in traffic and we erupt spontaneously. Evidence that the mind has a mind of its own and that we need to be aware of what it is up to. As an example, fearful ideas and feelings will sometimes emerge from our subconscious and in the absence of consciousness about our thinking, we are unable to discern what is true or false in those ideas and then they drive us.

We often think with our fears rather than with a clear and conscious mind and fear is the basis of much, if not all of our unproductive behavior. Fear is invariably the cause of inaction, disappointment, failure and it is certainly a factor in most, if not all illnesses. Ironically, most of our fear is not based on any real or immediate threat. Most fear is mental fear, caused by our mind taking past memory or experience, usually based on erroneous stories we have told ourselves, and then projecting those thoughts into future expectations. Expectations that will in most situations rarely materialize.

Children are able to demonstrate this fact all of the time. In one real life story, "bad people" were visiting a young boy during the night. His favorite uncle advised the child to just place his pants neatly on the end of his bed and it would "keep the bad people away." The uncle admitted to the boy that he didn't know how it worked, but he absolutely knew that it did work, because it always worked for him when he was a little boy. It worked again for that boy and later for his boy and then for his grandson. Then there was the young girl who repeatedly dreamed of being chased by the toy *Mr. Potato-head.* She was sent to bed with a potato masher and an explanation as to why potatoes feared the device. She never saw the scary toy again. The power of belief at work. The power of our thinking at work!

An additional aspect of low consciousness or decreased self-awareness is negative thinking. Thinking positively is of course not about denying the reality of life's stressors, but about looking at life objectively and searching for the positive within every life experience, while not negating life's challenges. Being aware of our thinking and learning to see the positive in events will cause us to see what some describe as the "inner dimension" of self.

As we develop greater awareness of our thinking and learn to direct that thinking we will see more and more evidence of the theory that "what we think, we become." But does that imply that we are responsible for, indeed that we cause everything that happens to us? Of course not. We can't control the weather for example, but we can control how we respond to the weather. Taking responsibility is different from being in control. If we take responsibility for our life, we may be able to influence many of the conditions that we experience, but obviously we cannot control all of the twists and turns that we will inevitably face. For example, we can take responsibility for our health, but we cannot control the ultimate outcome. We can make healthy choices, but good health is a complex thing based on many factors including some "cards we are dealt with," such as our childhood development, gender, culture, biology and genetics.

However, to allow ourselves to become a "victim" of circumstance and think that there is little we can do about many of these determinants of health is to fail to realize the power that we do have. We have an extraordinary ability to influence our environment and we also have the power to choose how we respond to the things we have no control over. Admittedly some of the determinants of our health are easier to assess or change than others, but there is action that is possible with each of them. We might say for example that we can't change our genetics or our development as a child. Well that is only partially true. Modern science is now telling us that even some aspects of our genetic composition can be changed over time. Identical twins at birth for example, can be very different by middle age. In addition, we can respond to our genetic makeup in ways that will influence it. For example, if our genetics leaves us predisposed to heart attacks or alcoholism, there are many choices we can make every day that can mitigate against or contribute to those outcomes.

Then there is child development. Many of us have stories we tell ourselves as a result of that experience; stories that are often false. Stories like I am no good, I am not smart enough, I am not talented enough or I am not likeable. Stories that need to be revisited understood and then abandoned. We cannot change our childhood, but we can change how we remember and respond to those experiences.

If we lack a consciousness of whom we are, clarity about what we want and an unwillingness to take action - all according to what we believe - life can never respond in our best interests. Putting a lot of thought and attention into something we don't want, but something we might fear and expect, may mean we will get that result. We will get what we expect to receive. So in order to attract what is best for us, we must be intensely aware of what we are thinking and that thinking must be in alignment with our belief system. If we don't think a result is achievable, it likely won't be. Believing is vital to success, which is probably why prayer, intention and even superstition tend to bring about results.

Most of us have muddled through much of our life not being aware that the way we were thinking may not have been the most advantageous to us. Through stillness we can learn a new way of thinking that will in turn provide a new consciousness of what is present, real and possible. That in turn will serve as a portal to maintaining or even ending a relationship.

Brain waves are a flow of energy which can be measured at anywhere from 1 to about 28 Hz. The slow brain waves, the *delta* waves, occur in deep sleep; *theta* waves occur when we are sleepy; *alpha* is a meditative or day-dreaming state, and beta occurs when we are thinking and intellectualizing. When our brain waves go into the *alpha state*, our heart rate slows, our breathing becomes deeper, we increase our oxygen intake, our intelligence increases and we secrete a whole range of different hormones. Some people will tell you that the "nature" of the mind is to be quiet. For most of us that is not so; there is incessant activity, chatter and static and a concerted effort must be made to slow it down.

A daily discipline of focused relaxation through the practice of meditation can give a person perspective, allowing them to become an impartial observer. The practice can provide a "bird's eye" view of problems, resources and the potential for greater success in our relationships. Meditation is not a "technique" and there is no right way to do it. Meditation is simply the art of just being – stopping and giving your mind a break. There are many ways to meditate, many guides in books and on the Internet – some prescriptive and some not. Find your own way.

Just find a comfortable spot to sit and close your eyes. Fix your attention on your breathing and be aware of the many thoughts that will try to rush into your consciousness. Don't try to force those thoughts out, but rather just bring your attention back to your breathing. By simply keeping your focus on your breath, you will get to the point of no thought. Another way of experiencing stillness is through techniques like the use of an electronic USB light and sound mind machine, through Yoga, or through "natural" ways to stillness such as with music, time with a pet or communing with nature. The state of "no thought" is considered a connection to "your divine being and energy body." It is a connection to all of your senses without analyzing, judging or even understanding what is happening. It is about moving away from everyday stresses and just "being."

Do you allow priority time for relaxing activities like sitting by water or fire? Do you have a routine and structured practice of daily meditation? Could periods of stillness help you see with greater clarity, perhaps leading to a more obvious decision about your future? Are you in tune what you are thinking, what you are feeling and how you affect others?

CHAPTER 10: DESTINY

"Control your destiny or someone else will."
                                    Anonymous

Former British Prime Minister Margaret Thatcher, known as the "Iron Lady," but also known for her personal consciousness, said that she lived the following philosophy: "Watch your thoughts, for they become words. Watch your words, for they become actions. Watch your actions, for they become habits. Watch your habits, for they become your character. And watch your character, for it becomes your destiny."

Were you destined to be in the relationship you are in? This is a true story. There was a young woman who lived in a small town in the north. She travelled to the city about 100 miles away (160km), in order to give birth to her son in a hospital. About two and a half years later another young woman travelled to the same hospital from about 30 miles away. She gave birth to a baby girl in the same hospital, in the same room and in the same bed. Neither women had ever met, however their husbands crossed paths regularly through their business interests. Twelve years later the first young woman who now had four children, grew tired of rural living and with her husband and family moved to a city in the south. Her husband was both a businessman and carpenter, so he purchased a small corner store and rented the adjacent apartment while he built a new family home.

A year later the second woman's husband found a new job in that same southern city. As the first family moved from the apartment at the back of the corner store, the second family moved in. Their "baby" girl, now aged ten, moved into the bedroom previously occupied by the "baby" boy, now aged twelve. The store was sold and the young girl's mother then worked in it for the new owners.

Over the next seven years the two children's paths would cross, but neither would pay much attention to the other. Then they both ended up working at the same location in a large organization. A romance was struck, the two married, had four children and they have now lived together for over fifty years. This story is not unique, with many people reporting similar "co-incidental" experiences. But is it more than co-incidence? Is there some kind of master plan? Was destiny at work?

Let's back up and ask the question about what destiny is. A common belief is that it is a pre-determined course of events produced by some external power, like a God. Others like William Jennings Bryan, a United States Presidential candidate in the late 1800's believed that "destiny is not a matter of chance, but of choice. Not something to wish for, but to attain." So are we at the mercy of our destiny, or was Bryan right?

The ancient Indian language of Sanskrit speaks of a destined love, kind of a karmic connection between two souls that are required by fate to meet and connect deeply. These legends say these destined souls recognize each other instantly by the sudden rapture they feel for the other person. It was believed that looks, movements, expressions, sounds, gestures and even scent enthralled them. The mythologies suggested that if we looked closely, we would recognize these beings by their lack of desire for others and by the wings that only they could see.

For many people, this concept of a "destiny" where decisions are made for us is unacceptable, because it implies a pre-determined result caused by something outside of us. That destiny would take away any ability for free choice. But if this Sanskrit "destined love" simply means that a God, the Universe or some other power may be providing an opportunity for connection and that we still need to "tune in" and decide, then the philosophy is closer to most modern western thought.

Many contemporary mystical writers and spiritual leaders accept the notion of a karmic connection between people. They see the development of relationships in terms of the choices we make as we move towards our destiny. That destiny they believe, is the final place that all humans arrive at after they have learned whatever they need to learn during their mortal life or lives. These spiritual teachers believe that there is a way for us to choose the conditions that will lead us towards having meaningful relationships, the connections that allow us to live a life of inspiration, contentment and prosperity.

While moving slowly during the consideration of "staying or going" can be a very wise approach, most of life's problems call for action earlier rather than later. Taking action requires a decision and a decision of great magnitude isn't usually easy. The reason for that difficulty is often fear. Will my decision be right? Will things work out? To a large measure, those answers may well depend on our attitude and expectations. Albert Einstein said we must all decide that the universe is either for us or against us. Not that the universe *is* for or against us, but that *we must decide* if it is for or against us. Remarkably, the universe is so accommodating that whatever decision we make, for or against, will begin to play itself out in our experience. The choice is ours.

When we are living in a difficult situation the worse place to be is in limbo. Presidential candidate William Bryan probably had it right when he said that our "destiny is a matter of choice." When making choices we should in most cases trust our intuition and expectations, because it is likely that the result of our decisions will be what we expect, rather than what we want. It is here that we must learn to think positively, to really expect life to deliver what will be best for us. To expect what will serve us best is not about failing to recognize some of our painful life experiences, but to see life as it is. If we exaggerate our resources, over-estimate our abilities, under-estimate our limitations and/or mis-read the threats in our world, we cannot accurately judge our experience. Even if we believe life is great, to misinterpret realities and facts will result in setting ourselves up for repeated disappointment and struggle.

Learning to be a positive thinker is not therefore about avoiding what is real, it is about looking at the "bright side," or perhaps more appropriately the "other side" of our experiences. Almost every occurrence has a positive dimension if we look for them. For example, we have an automobile incident, but no one is hurt. We are graded poorly on an assignment, but learn a great deal. We lose a job, but then we find a better one that we otherwise would not have looked for. We need an operation, but the surgical problem is correctable and we have medical insurance. We suffer a serious illness or accident and develop a whole new appreciation for life. We divorce, but then find a more loving compatible partner. One could initially look negatively at every one of these experiences and as a result develop an attitude of being a victim in life. Or one could accept "what is," learn from the experience and expect the best in the future. Thinking positively therefore, is really about reflecting on one's life and learning from experiences. It is an effortful practice involving the search for the full potential within every life occurrence. It is about facing - not about denying life's challenges.

Even with the greatest of expectations in mind, making a decision can be difficult when people are driven by fear. It is common to feel self-doubt and insecurity just before a major decision and it is at this juncture that people can learn to trust feelings and intuition by simply asking themselves a few illuminating questions about what they think the outcome of their decision might be. They shouldn't focus on the process or on their fears, but rather on an expectation of where they want the decision to eventually take them. Thinking about that outcome, they should ask themselves how they feel? Excited, passionate and open to possibilities or trapped and powerless? Do they feel joyful or anxious? Do they feel the decision is "right," or do they feel they are being "pushed?"

If individuals can think positively and "know in their heart" that a decision is right, it probably is. Unfortunately fears often come back and people feel like they can't take action - they feel immobilized. More thinking will not overcome that fear, but action will. That is the time to take one's mind off of the end result and think only of the next step. They now need to focus on what to do rather than how they feel. It may help to realize that once people act they usually feel elation. An exciting emotional high invariably occurs after people take the action they were afraid to take. Try to remember that feeling of elation after each decision and prior to your taking each step in your plan. As you do, you will build confidence and over time feel less and less fear.

Do you accept that all things begin with thought? Do you realize that thoughts lead to emotions and those feelings over time become your attitudes? Do you realize that most of life's inaction is driven by fear? Do you know that those attitudes drive your choices and your choices will become your destiny? Do you understand that in the final analysis, you will most likely be the architect of your destiny?

SECTION 3: *Universal Experiences*

CHAPTER 11: GENDER

"Men marry women with the hope they will never change. Women marry men with the hope they will change. Invariably they are both disappointed."

Albert Einstein

Many couples part company because they say they are not understood. Is understanding the opposite sex really possible, or is the notion of "understanding gender" an oxymoron; a noun that refers to contradictory words. In this case, "understanding" and "gender" would be contradictory for many, in that they would say men and women are simply beyond understanding each other. In the 1990's book "Men Are From Mars, Woman From Venus," author Dr. John Gray presented some stereotypical descriptions of men and women that offended some readers and academics, but sold 50 million copies of the book. Dr. Gray obviously "struck a chord" with the public when he made generalized yet compelling arguments as to the differences in the genders.

Dr. Gray argued that most of the relationship problems

between men and women are a result of fundamental psychological differences and a major thesis of the book deals with dissimilarities in the way men and women manage distress. We were told that men will withdraw temporarily, "retreating into their caves." They will often retreat literally, moving to a workshop or garage, or simply by visiting friends. In these "caves," men are not necessarily focused on the problem at hand, using the "time-out" in order to distance themselves from the situation and then later re-examine the problem from a new and fresh perspective. Conversely, Dr. Gray postulated that women preferred to talk with someone close about the problem, focusing on feelings rather than fixing. This scenario results in a dynamic where the man retreats as the woman tries to grow closer, obviously then causing conflict.

Another stereotype in the book is an articulation of how men love to have their abilities recognized and appreciated while women love to have their feelings recognized and appreciated. As a rule, men don't rate feelings highly because they "result in passionate unstable behavior." Conversely, women don't rate abilities as highly as feelings, because unequal abilities can result in "aggressive and competitive behavior."

Men like to work on their own, according to Dr. Gray, exercising their abilities by solving problems quickly and singlehandedly. Women like to co-operate and reveal their feelings through communication with one another. Men value solutions and view unsolicited assistance as undermining their efforts to solve problems alone. Women value assistance and will object to any advice that undermines their effort to proceed interactively. One of Dr. Gray's examples of this difference is the frequent male complaint that they offer solutions to problems raised by women and then they are told they misunderstood the message. The conclusion was that women aren't as interested in solving problems as they are in finding a place to "vent," to release emotions.

The general advice given by author Gray is for each gender to appreciate the differences and to stop expecting each other to act and feel the way the other does. The books critics will say that it simply plays into an outdated stereotypical and false pre-conception of masculinity and femininity. And the critics are probably right, at least partially. There are certainly women who prefer fixing to feeling and there are also women who prefer to solve problems independently and through introspection. And of course there are men who are excellent at expressing feelings and men who like to solve problems cooperatively.

However, notwithstanding the fact that society has changed considerably since Dr. Gray's book was published more than a quarter century ago and notwithstanding the need to recognize the danger of stereotypes, it seems quite obvious that most men and women still exhibit some very different characteristics. It might therefore be valuable to recognize how those differences have influenced your relationship. One method is to make an assessment of the following typecasts and then use or discard them as might seem appropriate.

First, let's look at feelings. Most men are what might be called "internal processors" and will deal with strong emotional events by first taking those feelings inside and working them to some solution before expressing them. Most women on the other hand are "external processors" and their feelings are more likely to be expressed outwardly, sometimes with enough emotion so as to be seen as "volcanic" by a mate. The man with no sensitivity to this difference may see the emotion as excessive and unwarranted, and will probably also complain that the response is not accompanied by any solving effort. The woman meanwhile may see the man's internal work as indicative of a cold indifferent attitude. They would both be wrong, as the couple would simply be using different processes to achieve the same end.

Then there is nurturing. Women as a rule are simply more nurturing. Man, who is historically the hunter, will probably be more interested in providing goods and services to the woman, whereas her inclination will be to look after the man emotionally. To a woman, loving means knowing and attending to the needs of others without waiting to be asked. Women tend to give unconditionally and actively seek ways to help others, whereas men tend to give when they think something specific is needed and then they expect their efforts will be appreciated.

Men tend to be much less sensitive than women in terms of deciphering what is needed without being specifically asked. Most highly expressive arguments involve an emotional disconnection rather than a disagreement on a particular issue. Men are usually relatively less attuned to the cues of tension and unhappiness in a partner and it is then common for the woman to express frustration that her distress is not being recognized. It is also then usual for the man to feel anger that he is being unfairly criticized. At that point the entire experience tends to become passionate and whatever issue may have precipitated the conflict is lost in emotion.

More dangerous than the emotional argument of course, is their avoidance. When that happens, men tend to do so by withdrawing inside themselves and refusing to talk while women are more inclined to pretend that the disagreement never happened. The issues are then likely to continue festering unresolved, eventually accumulating and triggering acting out in passive, aggressive or addictive behaviors. The reality of course is that disagreements can be a very positive aspect of any relationship if they can be managed respectfully and effectively.

In the past, the differences between men and women were defined by a society where men took a superiority position over women. In the current era of "equality" it is sometimes considered heresy to even speak of differences. There are of course physical differences between most men in both anatomy and physiology. Two simple examples are that men are generally better suited for force and physical confrontation; few women could play professional football. On the other hand, women have a different brain structure that allows them to more readily access both sides of the brain for problem solving.

There are also numerous psychological differences that may be difficult to see, but nonetheless seem to exist. Although not universal, these differences apply to most of us. To touch on a few additional variations, men seem more able to avoid personalizing a situation and can limit the number of issues they address, while women have a propensity to connect personally and to be perplexed by too many factors. Women seem to have a better memory for strong emotional experiences while men are more inclined to remember accomplishments. In relationships, men tend to prefer shared activities that are vigorous, exciting and sexual, while women tend to prefer more communication and intimacy in the experience.

In the final analysis, all of these differences need to be seen as oversimplifications and obviously do not apply to everyone, so to repeat a sentence from the outset,

make your personal assessment of the typecasts as they fit for you in your relationship and then use or discard them as might seem appropriate. In that context, there are two stereotypical generalizations that couples invariably report as being valid for them and that that you might want to consider in terms of your own relationship. *Women want to be valued for their beauty and perfection, they want to be listened to, heard and to have their feelings respected. Men on the other hand want to be viewed as strong and valued for what they say and do.* It may however be even more valid to describe what we all want. *To be valued for how we look, that we are listened to, that we feel respected and that we are appreciated for what we do.* The point here is that for relationships to flourish, men and women need to understand that there are differences, that our partner may not think and feel as we do and it is our job to understand and respect them and not to change them.

How is your partner different from you? Do you expect them to behave as you do? Do you accept their differences? Do they accept yours? Are those differences irreconcilable? Are you trying to change your partner?

CHAPTER 12: GEOGRAPHY

"Love, having no geography, knows no boundaries"

Truman Capote

Does where you live make a difference? Would your relationship be easier to maintain if you lived a simple rural life? Would your relationship be easier if you lived in a different part of the country?

Let's look at rural life first, where the expectations are changing. And so is the rural divorce rate. Rural Americans are now just as likely as city dwellers to have a marriage end in divorce. In the 1970's, the divorce rate was so low in some rural states that it resembled urban America in 1910. Rural dwellers tended to be churchgoers, women worked in the home and divorce was "taboo."

The current change in attitude appears to be due to both changing values and opportunities. Women are no longer expected to stay home and raise children, divorce is no longer as stigmatizing and more rural women have opportunities as a result of better education. Those factors make them less reliant on their husbands and this one element alone might result in an even greater number of separations in the future. But maybe not. College-educated Americans are more likely to get married and stay married than those with a high school diploma and while only about one in six rural residents now has a college degree in the United States, it is increasing annually.

So does where we live really make a difference? There are in fact geographic differences throughout the U.S. and across Canada. In 2018 in the United States, men and women in the southern states had the highest divorce rates while those in the northeast of both the U.S. and Canada had the lowest. Arkansas, Oklahoma and Kentucky had the highest rates in the U.S, while in Canada, the higher rates were in Alberta, British Columbia and Quebec, located in the west and central parts of the country.

Although these states and provinces have different rates - as do many cities - and although there are still small differences between city and country living, most research demographers believe that the variances are more attributable to the education, income and religious factors than they are to geography.

Notwithstanding, where we live in the country seems to still make some difference and people who choose rural living may have, or may have in the past had, some advantages over their urban counterparts. To acquire that advantage, we might need to look back at life in a time when rural divorce statistics were half of those of their urban counter-parts. We would then find - and in some regions of the country may still find - a lifestyle that seems simpler, less focused on purchases, less competitive and with fewer distractions. Rural dwellers were more likely to rely on each other for sustenance, entertainment and pure enjoyment of life.

The reality of course is that we can look back, but we probably can't go back to those times without living in a commune or in an exceedingly remote area of the country. And few would really want to. When the rural divorce rate was low, most families had very clearly defined gender roles; men were the head of the household and bread-winner and women stayed at home as the homemaker and child caregiver. The inaccessibility of transportation meant that many generations of families lived near one another or even under the same roof. The women managed most of the household tasks that were laborious, time-consuming and done by hand. Families had many children in order to help with farm labor and many of those children died from a range of diseases now commonly treated or even eradicated.

Over the years, industry and technology has made household tasks less time consuming and travel less difficult. Educational and employment opportunities have expanded and more importantly, attitudes have shifted about what professions are appropriate for women. Improved contraception lowered the number of children born and health-care improvements reduced mortality rates. Laws changed, challenging the discrimination of women and minority groups and probably most significantly, mass media and the Internet now influence most aspects of family life.

In conclusion, there were many disadvantages, but some plusses for relationships in the more rural area of the two countries and although separation rates are more attributable to other factors than they are to geography, there are some aspects of country life that we might learn from, behaviors that help nurture both parent and family relationships. We should therefore probably not search for a different part of the country to live in order to better maintain a relationship, but rather to look for what we can learn from country living in the past.

A part of looking at the past is to recognize that we are now a consumer society that buys much more than we really need and then we frequently discard the product in a short time. Social science research tells us that if we have the ability to get what we want, we still get greater enjoyment from wanting things than from getting them and then we get greater joy from the purchase than we do from owning and using. Think about the excitement generated by your last decision to buy a new vehicle. The actual purchase was probably a little less exciting and then ownership likely became mundane. Another significant change in our lives is the use of technology. Technology has contributed in numerous ways to our lives, but for some it has become all consuming.

So what can we do to return to that simpler life of the past without giving up the benefits of today? Do you take on one job at a time and do it well? Do you take time to unwind in a quiet place near nature and away from stimulation? Do you learn from failure; figure out what went wrong and do the task again? Do you acknowledge, support and care for your neighbors and friends? Do you purchase what you need or really want and are you discriminating and allow time to consider if the item is really required before a purchase? If the research is right and wanting gives more pleasure than having, do you want and enjoy?

Do you read all e-mail only once and deal with them right away if possible, handling the important stuff first, deleting the inbox once a week? Do you limit the time children spend on their smart phones? In fact, you should retain ownership of those phones and allow their use as a privilege. (Children should probably not "own" phones. If using a phone is a borrowed privilege, it is much easier to control its use.)

Do you realize that most things in life are best in moderation? That personal time with those around us is essential to maintaining relationships? Do you structure time for connecting? Do you have a consistent time for you, your partner and your family to meet and talk every day? (The dinner table is an ideal time and location to de-brief the day's activities, thoughts and feelings. No television allowed.)

Many couples complain that one partner is required to handle more of the day-to-day responsibilities than the other; do you share the workload? (Do you rely on your parent's division of labor? If you do, don't, negotiate your own division and help out.) Do you clarify roles, negotiate tasks and are you flexible in order to accommodate any unexpected challenge like a health concern?

CHAPTER 13: CULTURE

"A nation's culture resides in the hearts and in the soul of its people."

Mahatma Gandhi

Our culture serves as the foundation of our identity and therefore has a strong influence on all of our relationships. When we speak of the culture of a nation, organization or group, we are referring to a set of predominant attitudes and behaviors that describe the people. North America is a melting pot, or perhaps more accurately a "salad bowl" of different cultures, making it difficult to describe the North American culture, let alone explain how that culture influences and is influenced by separation rates.

It is generally believed that American culture began with the migration of people from North Asia over a land bridge from Siberia to current day Alaska thousands of years ago. Although the Vikings travelled to North America some 500 years before Columbus, the major influences in the United States came from English, Scottish, Welsh, Irish, German, French and Italian immigrants, with some influence by both Native and Latin American people. Those European cultures largely determined the Canadian culture as well, with somewhat more influence by the English and French.

As a result, both the United States and Canada have similar cultures with both conservative and liberal elements, although many Canadians view themselves as less assertive and more peace loving. For example, Canadians spend the bulk of their tax dollars on healthcare while the United States spends their money on the military. The political structures are also similar, with an ultimate value in democracy, a strong work ethic, competitiveness, risk taking, free expression, individualism, materialism and strong moral elements. Notwithstanding these commonalities among the people, both countries are diverse as a result of the large-scale migration from many ethnically and racially different countries throughout their history. This diversity includes birth, death and divorce rates.

In the United States, the once largest minority, African Americans, comprise almost 15 percent of the population and their homes are the least likely to contain a married couple. An African American child is also three times more likely to be born out of wedlock than a white child and on average, will spend about six years in a two-parent family compared with thirteen and fourteen years respectively for a Hispanic or Caucasian child. While marriage has become a less common choice throughout America, the numbers are even more dramatic for African Americans. Similarly, the rates of divorce, separation, cohabitation, out-of-wedlock births and children residing in female-headed households have all increased.

In Canada the French minority comprises about 22 percent of the population and until the late 1960's, divorce was virtually unheard of. Staunchly Roman Catholic, most of the population was influenced by religious leaders who condemned the practice. Then the laws changed to allow "no fault" divorces, where the rules no longer required a wrongdoing by either party in order to dissolve a marriage. About the same time, post war attitudes shifted and as the Church's influence over the population waned, couples began to separate in large numbers. Although French statistics remain only slightly higher than other ethnic groups in the country, like black America the rates of divorce, separation, cohabitation, out-of-wedlock births and children residing in female-headed households have all increased.

Hispanics, now America's largest minority, are increasing in numbers each year as couples demonstrate a strong value on family and therefore have more children than other racial and ethnic groups. These values include emphasizing the needs of the group rather than of the individual, loyalty, avoiding conflict, being self-sacrificing, showing perseverance and of course being religious. In most homes, gender roles remain clear, with the woman being responsible for morality and running the household while the man protects and provides. Probably as a direct result of these values, divorce rates are about 30 percent lower than for other racial and ethnic groups. Fewer couples cohabitate, there are fewer out-of-wedlock births and fewer children reside in female-headed households. The Latino population in Canada likely exhibit similar characteristics, however at less than two percent of the total population, statistical information is limited.

The Asian population in the United States, now at 5 percent, is only a third of the Canadian number at 15 percent. In both countries the Asian minority is growing quickly and with it comes a renewed emphasis on "family" values. In Asia, a marriage is not solely a relationship between spouses, but involves the extended family. Probably as a consequence of that factor, Asians have the highest rate of marriage and the lowest divorce rate of any racial and ethnic group in North America. They are generally also relatively well educated and financially successful, additional factors in fruitful relationships. But not all is well in many Asian households. The clash between Eastern and Western culture may be contributing to domestic violence that tends to be higher among Asians, where traditional attitudes toward marriage and gender roles perpetuate patriarchal norms of dominance and the corresponding strict control over women.

Then there are the American "First Nations" who top the separation statistics, as they seem to do in most every negative social classification. Comprising less than 1 percent of the U.S. population and slightly more than 4 percent in Canada, this is a race and culture with wonderful traditional values including veneration for the wisdom of elders, responsibility towards family and community, respect for the environment and a belief in sharing. But for centuries, the "white-mans" world has clashed against those values resulting in a culture that now appears to be broken. The combination of a higher percentage of women who are divorced with an increasing number of women who have never married, helps explain why more than any other race, First Nations children reside with a single parent or with grandparents.

North American citizens, whatever the ethnic group, whether African, Latino, Aboriginal, Asian, Caucasian or otherwise, find that relationship dissolution is now part of everyday life. It is embedded in laws and institutions, manners and mores. For most of the two nations' history, divorce was a rare occurrence and an insignificant feature of family and social relationships, but after 1960 it accelerated at a stunning pace. The laws changed of course, but what were the attitudes that supported those new laws?

Following the Second World War where 45 million civilians and 15 million soldiers died, the world's population seemed to take a second look at the meaning of life. Within a short period of time there appeared to be a widespread shift in thinking about life's offerings and obligations. The change was subtle, but it moved people away from an ethic of obligation to others and toward an obligation to self; a kind of entitlement to the good life, whatever its length. People seemed to become more acutely conscious of their responsibility to attend, if not to their own individual needs and interests, to that of their children's needs and interests. What followed were generations of young people raised within a culture of entitlement and greater self-interest. Combined with relative affluence and new resources through much of North America, this shift had a profound impact on ideas about the nature of the family.

Academics, the media, recreational drugs and new generations of "entitled" youth represented the parts of life devoted to the pursuit of individual interest, choice, and freedom, while the concept of the family represented an expectation of commitment, duty, and self-sacrifice. What people seemed to want was a family that supported aspiration and advantage rather than service and sacrifice. This change in attitude eventually resulted in a new cultural concept of divorce linked to the pursuit of individual satisfaction with life. So if one is dissatisfied, one just moves on.

It seems clear therefore that one's culture has an effect on relationship estrangement rates. But only if the individual did not immigrate to North America at too early an age, because children who immigrate later in life are more likely to have absorbed home country values from their ethnic communities. As detailed earlier, there are many factors that influence divorce and separation rates such as the age at marriage, economic status, educational achievement, income, parental divorce, and even whether the union was a first, second, or third marriage. Other factors include premarital cohabitation and childbearing, economic stress, poor communication and infidelity.

By examining these factors in cultures that have lower separation and divorce rates, we can learn from their experiences and then perhaps replicate some of the reasons for their lower numbers. One of our biggest challenges is finding a community where the members are socially integrated in supportive and structured environments for recreation, socialization, education and worship. Do you live in such a community?

CHAPTER 14: RELIGION

"My husband and I divorced over religious differences. He thought he was God, and I didn't."

Unknown

When does religion help a relationship? Perhaps when it is actually practiced. The research and literature on religion and separation/divorce contain some very conflicting conclusions. On the one-hand some studies have concluded that the more fundamental the Christian, the more likely they are to divorce. Equally disturbing is that when those couples experience a divorce, many of them feel their community of faith provides rejection rather than support and healing, raising important questions about the effectiveness of how churches minister to families.

Residents of both the American and Canadian northeastern sea-board are commonly noted for their more liberal leanings in politics and lifestyle, however the regions of the two nations in which divorce is lower than the average is precisely in those "liberal" areas. Conversely, Evangelical Christians who make up about 25 percent of the U.S. population and 10 percent of the Canadian numbers, have higher divorce rates than the population over-all. The annual rates in Newfoundland, New York, New Jersey and Vermont for example, are between 9 and 10 divorced individuals for every thousand people, while

Arkansas, Alabama, Kentucky and Oklahoma have 15 to 17 per thousand. The white conservative Protestants along with their black Protestant neighbors are statistically more likely than the average American to separate, including those people who claim no religion. It seems therefore that the common conservative argument that "strong religion leads to strong families" may not hold up.

The so-called "Bible belt" professes to be pro-marriage and the statistics must be troubling to them. Or perhaps not. Religious organizations counter these studies with their own figures that suggest divorce statistics would be higher in so called liberal states if more people married rather than just lived together. They also point to their own studies that claim divorce rates are lower with practicing Christians who attend church weekly and pray together daily. In one such study they concluded that couples that were active in their faith were actually less likely to divorce than their neighbors. And the numbers varied by religion. Catholic couples were 31 percent less likely to divorce, Protestant couples 35 percent less likely and Jewish couples 97 percent less likely.

People in the Jewish faith do have a lower rate of divorce at 30 percent, even though they recognized the concept of "no-fault" divorce thousands of years ago. Judaism generally maintained that it was better for a couple to divorce than to remain together in a state of constant bitterness and strife, but traditionally it was there that the liberal attitudes ended. In the Orthodox Jewish belief, the man would have to make the decision to divorce - or to allow the divorce. The divorce rules were taken from the "Talmud," a written record of the historic opinions and teachings of pre-Christian Rabbis. Now largely viewed as historical tradition, the policies no longer fit well with contemporary values. In those Jewish traditions, women would have to appear before a rabbinical court in order to obtain permission to separate, yet a man could divorce a woman for most any reason, or for no reason. The Jewish rules specifically decreed that a man could divorce a woman because she spoiled his dinner or simply because he found another woman more attractive. In addition, the Jewish faith did not recognize civil divorce, so separating couples that used a civil procedure still had to be careful to have their dissolution recognized by their Synagogue in order to avoid living in another "adulterous" relationship. In modern North America, people who live by some Jewish traditions may still obtain a "get" - a formal religious document that specifies a marriage is over - but increasingly, subscribers to the faith are just using a civil arrangement.

Members of the Muslim faith in the middle-eastern countries have a very low divorce rate, which is understandable in the context that the prophet Mohammed is said to have decreed: "Of all the lawful acts the most detestable to Allah is divorce." It is also notable that separations are usually initiated by fundamental male followers of the faith and in some countries that results in dire consequences for women. Less rigidly orthodox Muslim countries like Turkey and Egypt have slightly higher divorce rates than others at about 10 percent. In North America, Muslim divorce rates are about the same as those in the Jewish tradition at about 30 percent. As with Jews, Muslim males have historically dominated the process and their top reasons for divorce are reported as being related to unacceptable in-laws, adultery and "haram" sex. (Any sinful act forbidden by Allah.)

A few years ago leaders of several large Christian churches described a large study by an American market research firm specializing in religious beliefs and behaviors as "controversial and disturbing." The research firm claimed that of all of the Christian churches they studied, the Baptists had the highest rate of divorce and the Lutherans the lowest, although the Mormon Church also had similar low rates. The non-denominational churches like the Centers for Spiritual Living had even higher divorce rates than the Baptists, however their level of acceptance and support of divorced members was better than most other religious organizations. Agnostics, or nonbelievers had the lowest rates of divorce in the study.

Dr. Bradford Wilcox, Director of the American "National Marriage Project," a research initiative originally based at the University of Virginia, is responsible for investigating how marriages are formed, maintained and ended and how society is affected. The project gathers statistical information and analyzes it to provide public education and to formulate recommendations for the future. Dr. Wilcox confirmed that conservative Christians really are divorcing more than people in other mainstream religious traditions and indeed more than people who have no religious affiliation at all. But Wilcox also said that "nominal" Christians who don't actively practice their faith and who rarely or never attend church affected the figures.

Other studies have avoided the controversy of how fervent church members may be by focusing on sociological issues. Evangelical Protestants they will argue, promote a culture of early marriage and the discouragement of birth control and higher educational attainment. It is those factors they conclude that drive the rates of separation up.

Many marriage counselors have a different take on the issue, noting that fundamentally religious people are often naive about the rigors and demands of a marriage relationship. Others engage in "fantasy thinking," waiting for God to fix their problems rather than using the religion as a source of moral strength. The atheist they will note, doesn't believe in God and so they must get on with doing the work themselves.

Followers of the Jewish or Muslim faiths should look behind the reasons for lower divorce rates; reasons that are a result of sociological factors that may not ultimately benefit the participants at all. Some examples are historic laws and writing interpretations that allow for male dominance, discrimination, inequality, harshness and even violence.

Because early marriage, poverty, the absence of birth control, poor education and naivety about the demands of marriage are factors known to affect separation rates, perhaps parishioners need to look carefully at the advice their spiritual leaders may be giving them about social and cultural factors. Those are admittedly dimensions of service that may be quite outside the purely spiritual belief in a God, but if the church wants to be of real help, those aspects of service must really be in the interests of parishioners and not of some unfounded dogma. Only then will the old adage "strong religion leads to strong families" be truly right.

So what does all this mean to people trying to make a decision about staying or going? If you belong to a church or spiritual center of some form, look to see if the values include a loving inclusive philosophy that guide and support a relationship. Or conversely, that guide and support a dissolution. But be wary of religions driven by leaders who promulgate sociological factors that destabilize relationships. Some examples are sex education that promote only abstinence, poor availability of contraceptive devices or pharmaceuticals, pressure for early marriage at a young age and stigma associated with cohabitation.

A faith group can be a powerful buffer against separation and divorce, or it can be an aid and support if the dissolution of a relationship is unavoidable. Or not! It is important therefore, to realize that a decision about staying or leaving can be strongly influenced and affected by your spiritual beliefs and connections.

CHAPTER 15: LAWS

"Marriage is really tough because you have to deal with feelings.....and lawyers."
                              Richard Pryor

Although more and more people are choosing to live together "common-law" there are still thousands of traditional marriages every year. When people do decide to marry, most of them tend to think of their plan as a social custom more than a legal process. In many instances great effort goes in to planning a grand event with very little, or no thought at all, into what they are really getting into. The second part of that fact also applies to most people who just move in together. What rights and responsibilities will they be assuming and in the event the union fails, what will the consequences be? With rare exception, virtually no thought goes into the possibility of separation or divorce. That would be "bad luck" or "bad intention."

If you asked someone to define marriage, what is the likelihood they would answer something like this: "Marriage in North America is the legal recognition of a union between two people that carries with it certain social and economic benefits, along with certain rights and responsibilities?" Probably not very likely at all. But that is exactly what it is. In the United States marriage is governed by the individual states while in Canada the national government has the lead role.

When considering a "stay or go" decision, a wise couple should know what laws will affect them and how. The U.S. complexity can make it a huge challenge, particularly if one moves from state to state.

And the laws relating to a common law relationship are even more complex. The term "common-law" typically refers to couples that live together in an arrangement that is like a marriage, but without an actual ceremony and without a legal document. In 2015, a common-law relationship could be contracted for in eleven of the U. S. states, although the requirements in each state were different. For example, one state recognized the arrangement for questions of probate only, one state recognized the union if it had been validated by another Court, two states recognized same sex common law relationships and 13 states simply prohibited any form of "common law" marriage at all.

Interestingly, common law relationships are recognized by the U.S. Federal government for tax purposes, if the arrangement is recognized by the state where the taxpayer lives, or in the state where the common-law marriage began. Effective in 2015, the "job protection" and "leave" provisions of the Federal Family and Medical Leave Act also applied to common law relationships in States where the statutes "are legally recognized." There are no provisions in any State for a common law "divorce."

Although Canada has a national Divorce Act making the common law provisions not nearly as complex, there are details that vary across the country and they tend to be poorly understood and sometimes get people into serious financial difficulties. The misunderstandings include a belief that the rules are the same in every jurisdiction and that in the event of breakup assets are divided, that spouses are entitled to support and that having children doesn't affect the rules. Wrong on all counts. For example, one province grants common-law partners all of the rights enjoyed by married couples after 2 years. In most others it is 2 or 3 years unless a child is living with the couple. Only one province won't recognize common-law relationships at all, while another has laws that are quite prescriptive, requiring an equal split on property, assets and debts. Two provinces disallow any division of assets and the remainder provide for a division if both parties have contributed towards buying those assets. Only one province has automatic child support, however child and spousal support can be granted by a Court of Law in all of the provinces.

While few people might be able to define marriage, they would probably do better describing divorce and it might go something like this: "Divorce is a legal process in which a judge dissolves a partnership and restores a couple to single status." What they might not add is this: "the process might include matters of spousal and child support, child custody and distribution of property, other assets and debt."

Laws differ greatly by jurisdiction and they are constantly changing, so couples should look carefully at their local rules. In fact, marriage laws have been altered rather dramatically over the years. Two significant changes were the removal of bans on inter-racial and same gender marriages. Polygamy, or the marriage to more than one person at the same time remains illegal throughout North America and has not changed for decades, although there are those who would propose that those laws should be made more liberal on the basis of freedom of choice.

The age at which people marry has changed over the years as well, with the median age now near 25 and 30 for women and men respectively, while 50 years ago the median age was 20 for women and 23 for men. Adults of any age can marry in most States and all provinces and most jurisdictions will allow 16 and 17 year olds to marry with parental consent.

The laws respecting divorce have also changed dramatically over the past century. Like marriage, divorce law in the United States rests with the individual State and therefore varies across the country, although there is remarkable consistency. Prior to the 1970's, a spouse seeking divorce in most states had to show a "fault" such as abandonment, cruelty, incurable mental illness or adultery. And even in those cases a judge might deny the divorce if he believed one of the parties contributed to the others "fault," as in encouraging adultery. A divorce might also be denied if there was "evidence" of forgiveness, such as continuing to live with a person. In some cases, lawyers would negotiate "uncontested" divorces, an arrangement that was significantly more private for the divorcing couple.

Then in the late 60's as public attitudes shifted and the so-called "sexual revolution" began, the concept of a "no-fault" divorce took root in Oklahoma and California. All states say that they now allow no fault divorce proceedings, although New York State "dragged its feet" and didn't pass enabling legislation until 2010. The "No-fault" criteria include irreconcilable differences, irretrievable breakdown, incompatibility or simply a period of living apart. Some States require a period of legal and/or physical separation prior to a formal divorce decree and although advertised as "no fault," in certain respects it is not quite so. For example, most states will take behavior into account when determining issues of child custody and support, spousal support and the fair distribution of family assets and debts.

The Canadian evolution of marriage and divorce law was also a bit convoluted. Although the Federal government now applies a uniform approach across the country, that was not the case prior to 1968. Each province had some semblance of law except for Quebec where the Catholic Church had great influence. In that province a person wishing a divorce had to apply to the Canadian Senate for a private Bill of Divorce where a special committee would undertake an investigation. Believe it or not, if the application had merit in the opinion of government officials, the marriage still had to be dissolved by an actual Act of Parliament.

The Canadian Divorce Act of 1968 allowed divorce for reason of adultery, marriage breakdown, physical or mental cruelty or simply living apart for a year. It was essentially a "no-fault" divorce law. The Act also set out the rules for custody and child and spousal support and then the provinces were charged with administering the Act. That is where differences occur, with the decisions about child custody, property division, education and mediation, potentially all being different.

Marriages in both countries can be religious or civil, performed by a member of the clergy or a representative of the courts like a Justice of the Peace, but all divorces must be Court sanctioned. The marriage of homosexual couples continues to be a controversial issue in many regions, although by 2015 it was allowed in all Canadian provinces and in 36 American states. There is at least one area where most state/provincial governments are in agreement however and that is in recognizing the chaotic and stressful nature of divorce, resulting in most jurisdictions having introduced less adversarial approaches to settlements such as mediation.

In spite of these complexities, beyond the marriage license or perhaps an event liquor permit, very few people even think about laws when they get married. They just don't think forward to the "bigger picture" and that's probably quite understandable. We get married for a variety of reasons. In surveys, people consistently say that they marry for love, companionship, commitment, continuity, security, permanence and to have children. They also acknowledge that they marry due to social pressure, for social legitimacy, in rebellion, to validate an unplanned pregnancy or to obtain legal entrance to a country. None of this speaks specifically to rights, responsibilities and potential consequences. We just don't think about those issues, at least not in the beginning.

Couples planning a separation need to look carefully at the laws where they live in order to address any issue that might arise in the future. As an example, child and spousal support (sometimes referred to as alimony or maintenance) were traditionally paid by a husband to an ex-wife. In recent years, the move towards gender equality has resulted in some husbands obtaining support from their former wives. Child support, where one parent contributes to the raising of their children by supporting the primary caregiver, is a particularly complex matter. The amount a person is required to pay varies by jurisdiction, with some being very prescriptive while others are quite inexplicit. If you live in Texas for example, you must have been married or lived together over 10 years in order to get support and payment amounts are usually limited to three years. In 2015 a spouse and child could not ask for more than $2,500 or 40 percent of gross income, whichever was less. In contrast, New York judges have only vague guidelines and that gives them huge discretion to determine both amount and duration.

Although divorce is considered "no fault" in most states, a judge in many of them can consider who might be at fault for the divorce in his decision regarding the level of support payments and at least one state is quite precise about that. In Georgia a person who commits adultery is not entitled to support payments at all. There are many other differences state to state, for example if you live in Utah, support is limited to the number of years you were married or lived together and if you live in Tennessee support is limited to half of the years together, while in Kansas you are only required to support a family for 121 months.

In Canada, the support arrangements, like the divorce laws, are considerably more consistent across jurisdictions than they are with their neighbors to the south. Although both married and common-law spouses may be entitled to spousal support, as indicated earlier, an important distinction between the two is that common-law relationships are governed by provincial statutes. In both divorce and common-law separations, the courts determine support levels by looking at time together and the functions performed by each spouse. In doing so, a judge will look for any economic advantage or disadvantage arising from the breakdown, any obligations in support of the children, relief of any economic hardship and the promotion of economic self-sufficiency in both parties.

Because Canadian law is "no fault," infidelity has no effect on payments. There are support level guidelines, but no specific formula for the level or duration of support. Awards for support can be time limited or indefinite, although in many cases a "review order" will allow reconsideration of any decision after a specific period of time. The guidelines used by judges are somewhat complex and awards will vary depending upon the custody agreement, number of children, net family income and so on, Higher income spouses will typically pay a higher percentage of income, because in theory it will pose less of a hardship than would a similar percentage with a lower income earner.

Complex and differing laws regarding marriage, common-law relationships, divorce, no-fault divorce, custody, child and spousal support provisions, asset division, debt distribution and other matters can have life-long implications. Before deciding to "stay or go," have you ensured you know and understand the laws in your jurisdiction? Have you considered the need for a lawyer?

SECTION 4: The Pressures

CHAPTER 16: MONEY

"My mother always said don't marry for money, divorce for money."
Wendy Liebman

There are at least five dimensions to the issue of money and relationships. The first question is whether or not you married for money. The second question is if there was money, was it combined within the relationship or kept separately. Thirdly, did money help or hinder your relationship? Fourthly, do you fight over money? And finally, what is a separation likely to cost in dollar terms?

For half of those in relationships, a separation is as common as was getting together. And the conjunction of emotion and money is powerful at both ends of those experiences. The two events are also likely to determine the standard of living for some time into the future, particularly if there are children involved, a frequent scenario.

Getting together for money! It is obvious from the statistics that a union based on love doesn't come with a guaranteed fairy-tale ending, although most people in our culture have been taught that love is the only good reason for marriage, or even just living together. There are related motivations of course - like having children - but many of us were told that the essential core of any relationship needed to be romantic love. Many of us were also told that love has always been the reason that people marry, but even a cursory look at history and cultures tell us that is not the case. Prior to the last century, people married for much more pragmatic reasons like sex, procreation, finances and companionship. In many places there were few partners to choose from and in other situations the relationships were "arranged" by families, which really meant, "assigned" by families. In summary, it was more common in the past to marry for something other than love.

Interestingly, recent studies have concluded that even today, relationships are more lasting if the motivation for the partnership is other than love; or at least, in addition to love. For example, to have children with someone we believe would be a good co-parent, to have financial security, or to have companionship. They are choices made with a purpose rather than from a poorly understood emotion called love. Additionally, the people in those studies described what was probably a more realistic expectation from the union. Their partner didn't need to be perfect, only good. If love was part of the equation, that was a bonus, but it would have to evolve in the future.

In the 1800's some people began to talk about marrying for love and according to the literature at the time, others expressed caution that the attitude would lead to unstable marriages. One of the problems they reasoned was that love was a changeable emotion and it seems they may have been right. People describe, "falling in love," but they also "fall out of love." There are many cards and posters that proclaim, "All You Need is Love," but anyone who has really looked at life and relationships know that is not the case. Unless of course one is of the view that with love, other needs will be met naturally.

Whatever one's view of love, if you put the concept in or take it out of the relationship equation, there are still many other needs. The need for respect, support, sex, shared goals, shared interests, understanding and a myriad of other psychological requirements. There is also a need for housing, food, transportation and other physical necessities. So if we marry for love, love is still not "all that we need."

The logical mind then might say that if one wants a successful relationship, the odds are better if one gets together for purpose rather than love, but that's not to say love couldn't or shouldn't be part of the equation. As an extension of that thought, one might argue that money is a "purpose" and therefore marrying for money is a better idea than marrying for love. Targeting money it would seem, would also be more strategic. But for most of us, the thought of finding a rich partner without the strong feelings of love seem quite empty. So whether logical or not, perhaps in North American culture it still makes more sense to "marry the love of your life" and then set a strategy of building wealth together.

Combining assets! Some couples become enthralled with each other very early in a relationship, operating within what might be described as a "romantic stupor." They may share or invest in property or other capital assets and then when the relationship fails they have trouble extricating themselves from the arrangement. In most cases they eventually find that it was a bad idea to combine assets early in a relationship before a solid commitment to the future was made. If and when that commitment is made, there are still two considerations to the question of "combining assets." The first is whether people should get married at all in terms of costs – such as tax burdens - and the second dimension is related to the simple combining of assets including bank accounts. From a purely economic point of view, older couples with significant resources should look carefully at marriage. In the United States for example, taxpayers with combined income of over $200,000 are hit hard by regular taxes and then get a double whammy by a federal tax, the Alternative Minimum Tax (AMT) designed to tax high-income earners. As an example, two taxpayers, living in Ohio, earning a total of $200,000 with typical deductions, would after getting married in 2012, pay an additional "marriage penalty "of about $15,000 in combined state and AMT assessments.

That is not the case however for low-income earners where the benefits are in favor of marriage. In California for example, a single person earning $40,000 a year, again with typical deductions, would pay about $6,000 in taxes while a married individual would pay about $5,000. Taxes vary in every state and every province and it may be that for some people, marriage was worth the extra cost, but in most cases people have never considered those realities, so meeting with an accountant before a lawyer might be a very useful thing to consider.

Although the lack of money does cause tension in a relationship, the lack of compatible values and goals regarding money is usually even more troublesome. There are some aspects of a relationship where "opposites attract," but one's view about money is not one of them. For example, if one person is a saver and the other is a spender, or if one believes in paying as you earn while the other prefers credit, or if one lives for today and the other is focused on the future.

In all of those situations, a "prenuptial agreement," setting out rules about the marriage should probably have been considered. Although some people will argue that prenuptial agreements imply distrust and can negatively affect a relationship, in recent years they are more common and therefore better accepted as "normal" practice. They are especially popular among spouses who have accumulated a substantial fortune or specific assets they wish to protect for others.

While these agreements are commonly referred to as prenuptial agreements, in Canada they are legally referred to as domestic contracts. The agreements can deal with any number of marital issues, including ownership and division of property, support obligations, the right to direct the education and moral training of children, or any other matter in the settlement of the spouses' affairs. In other words, the two parties agree in advance on their respective rights and obligations within the marriage, during any separation or annulment, or as a result of death. What can be wrong with that?

The answer to the third question of whether having some money helps vaccinate us from separation is somewhat clearer. It is important to recognize that two people living together usually means greater household income and single parents experience a poverty rate significantly higher than couples. For example, the lone parent median income in 2013 was $40,000 in Canada and even lower at $26,000 in the U.S. In contrast, the median income for a married couple in 2014 varied by state and province, but hovered around $84,000 in the U.S. and $77,000 in Canada.

One recent study found that couples with incomes of $100,000 or more had lower divorce rates than those with less money. Another study concluded that individuals with annual incomes of more than $50,000 had a lower chance of divorce than those who earn less than $25,000. Yet another study concluded that rising debt after a couple's union contributed to arguments and eventually to instability and in some cases separation or divorce. In the couples that reported disagreeing about finances, both men and women identified financial problems as the most serious and destructive in their relationships. Couples who argued more than once a week were thirty percent more likely to divorce than couples that reported disagreeing about finances only a few times a month. Of all the things couples fight about, and there are many, money disputes are apparently the best predictor of a relationship failure.

Poor finances are stressful and apparently having a good income can be a form of preventive immunization, helping couples avoid tensions that lead to yet more problems. In one five-year study of the "habits of the rich and poor," the research team reported that 87 percent of the wealthy were happy in their marriage, while only 47 percent of the poor were happy. The study reported that being rich eliminated the distress associated with money problems and that in turn improved overall health.

In another highly publicized 2010 study reported in Time Magazine, researchers found that lower income did not cause problems in itself, but made people feel more "ground down" by the problems they had, and that in turn caused anxiety and depression. However, at an annual earning of $75,000 that effect seemed to disappear. It is likely that at the $75,000 level - in 2019, now closer to $95,000 if you apply the inflation rate - people probably have enough expendable cash to avoid distress from just trying to make "ends meet." The money also allows a bit of freedom to do some of the things they like to do. In summary, earning up to the magic mark that allows freedom and less stress is important, but earning a lot more likely does little to help the relationship. Wealth brought other issues like worry over losing one's money, not being able to maintain the same lifestyle in retirement, feeling guilty about having much more than others, competing with other wealthy friends and so on. In summary, anxiety about money.

It is also true that income is relative. That is, a person's satisfaction with their level of income is partly related to the income of those around them. Being poor is more difficult if you are the only poor family on the block.

What is the cost of separation? The answer to the question regarding the financial cost of separation and divorce also has several dimensions. There is of course the splitting of assets and Court judgments regarding support payments, dealt with in more detail in chapter fifteen on the law, where a typical scenario is detailed. In that example, a husband, earning $100,000 a year with a stay-at-home wife who has custody of two children, would pay about $1,200 per month in child support and $2,300 in spousal support. In addition, he might be required to pay for medical and dental care, educational costs, extracurricular activity like sports and music lessons and so on. After taxes the husband in this scenario would need to live on about $3,000 a month, a little more than one-third of his gross income. As explained in that chapter, laws vary by jurisdiction and the specific outcomes depend on many factors, but the bottom line, regardless of where one lives, is that separation and divorce will be costly.

There are also other important systemic issues to consider as part of a separation decision. As a rule, women will suffer more. They are usually the ones who take custody, or at least provide primary care to the children and as a result set their careers aside. The implications of shelving a career can be long lasting, but the short-term consequences are also great. Although statistically outdated by a decade, the ratios probably haven't changed that much, where in 2009 divorced men in the U.S. enjoyed median incomes of $75,000 while women languished at half that amount, although support payments in some cases served as the great equalizer. Statistically, women in America still make one-third the money that men make over their life span and one in five women live at the poverty level after retirement.

So if you are now looking at a separation, you need to examine a few important questions. Are there significant assets? What are the implications for taxation? Did you keep your assets separate? Do you share the same values on saving and spending? Do your spending and communication patterns often lead to bickering? Finally, do you recognize the extraordinarily high financial cost of separation? Will the cost of leaving be worth it?

CHAPTER 17: INFIDELITY

"If another woman steals your man there is no better revenge than letting her keep him. Authentic men can't be stolen."

Unknown

A few years ago a young lady leased a 24X12-foot billboard along a major train commuter route in a large eastern American city. The billboard read:

*"Hi Steven,
Do I have your attention now?
I know all about her. You dirty, sneaky, immoral, unfaithful, poorly endowed slime-ball. Everything's caught on tape.*

*Your (soon to be ex)wife
Emily
P.S. I paid for this billboard from our joint account."*

Might Emily and Steven reconcile? Not this week. Being cheated on hurts. Optimists will declare that "anything is possible," but rebuilding trust after an affair is very difficult. The hurt feelings from an act of infidelity remain for a long time. The initial reactions of resentment, disgust and bitterness are usually accompanied by a loss of trust and it is that feeling that studies predict, might take a minimum of five years to repair, if ever.

One might think that an emotional connection with a third person would be more threatening to a spouse than a sexual tryst, but that somehow doesn't seem to be the case. The sexual nature of an affair is often the most difficult to overcome. It rarely matters if the act was "a fling," perhaps an indiscretion fueled by drugs or alcohol. And those kinds of events are not uncommon. It is believed that more than a majority of married individuals will engage in infidelity at some point in their relationship. In the past, men were more likely to have affairs, but recent surveys show the rate for men and women to be similar. Interestingly, most of the people who "cheat," claim to be happy in their relationships.

Happy or not, relationship deceit will ultimately destroy a partnership and it is almost always discovered. Just ask the subscribers to the *Ashley Madison* web site that caters to married people, offering a "safe" way for them to be involved in extra-marital sexual activity. In 2015 a web based vigilante group hacked into the company's database and publicized the names of their clients. Thirty million of them worldwide, and Ashley Madison is only one of dozens of dating sites, albeit the largest. The publicity resulted in political scandal, suicides, fear of reprisal, blackmail and predictions of major work opportunities for divorce lawyers across the U.S and Canada. The publicity certainly added credibility to surveys that estimate 60 percent of North Americans are involved in extra-marital experiences at some point in their relationship.

Wherever or whatever happens to these thirty million "members," one thing is predictable, their "significant others" will view the activity as a betrayal of trust - a lack of faithfulness. And it is. In some cases, the relationship will already be rocky and the affair will only reinforce the unstable nature of the union. In other cases, the relationship might have been relatively strong, but the indiscretion will arouse doubts about all past perceptions of the union. "Why wouldn't he have told me that there was something wrong with our marriage?" "How could I have been so blind, so stupid, not to notice anything?" "Doesn't she love me?" "Did he ever love me?" "If I stay here it will only be for the kids!" "I am done!" The angry questions and conclusions will typically roll around people's head incessantly for what will seem like forever.

So why do individuals, many in loving relationships, "play around?" The reasons may lead us to understand what chances there are for reconciliation. One reason is the simple attractiveness of youth. As people age and begin to feel less desirable, the beauty of youth can be seductive and if an opportunity for sex arises, it can be difficult to ignore. The Internet with its ready access and promises of privacy and confidentiality can be particularly tempting. In many cases, the place where bad decisions are made is not driving down to the local "strip," but on that Internet or even more likely, back at work where more than sixty percent of affairs start.

Sexual relief is a biological need and it demands to be satisfied. In some people the need feels as urgent as the need to urinate and if relief is not available at home, while readily available elsewhere, the outcome will be predictable. But are they all "bad decisions," or are some genetically driven? Two American studies suggest there may be a link between genetics and monogamy. It may be kind of like alcoholism where the individual has a predisposition towards certain behaviors. In the animal world, most males are genetically programmed to propagate by mating with as many females as possible. There are a few species of rodents like the prairie vole that stick with one mate throughout their life, raising offspring and protecting the family against predators. Interestingly the prairie vole's relative, the meadow vole, mates with as many females as possible and then heads for the next meadow location.

Researchers found that the prairie vole had a different brain function with more of a protein called the vasopressin receptor. Using gene therapy, the researchers added extra receptors to the brain of the meadow vole. Apparently it turns out he then became much more like his cousin and remained with a mate. The same result was obtained in research with monkeys whose genetics are even more closely related to humans. The implications of this work - should it be proven to apply to humans - is that genetic make-up affects monogamy and by extension could affect separations. It might not be wise however, to use the excuse that you strayed because you are related to the meadow vole, because the view that you are a vole or rodent might be accepted quite readily. One might also not want to expect any understanding that your decision was beyond your control.

Other than the controversy of genetic make-up, a better understood driver of infidelity is boredom or dissatisfaction within the marriage itself. Boredom that often comes from a pre-occupation with the routine demands of life, while ignoring the relationship needs. We focus on responsibilities rather than what might be fun. Vacuuming that floor for example, becomes more important than a "date night."

Dissatisfaction with a relationship is often transient and comes from familiarity, feelings of being misunderstood or poor communication. The thoughts can sometimes lead to "innocent" friendship relationships with other members of the opposite sex. The initial platonic exchange however will often result in deep personal sharing that will with few exceptions, eventually result in a liaison of infidelity. Any discussions that undermine or criticize a partner or aspects of a primary relationship will prove to be a very "slippery slope" and should be taken as signs of relationship problems that need to be addressed with one's partner – and quickly.

There are of course no valid excuses for violating a trust commitment to another person, but there are reasons and careful examination of those reasons could lead to reconciliation. There may also be factors external to the primary relationship that need to be considered before any decision is made to terminate. For example, if there are children involved, it may well pay to make an extra effort to save the relationship. The short-term pain may be worthwhile in order to prevent the chaos and hurt that the family will surely experience.

Believe it or not, in some situations an act of infidelity can lead to a more loving and nurturing relationship. If one can treat the infidelity as a catalyst, the damage can be addressed and bring with it a new appreciation of the affiliation. When an emotional storm occurs, people are inclined to address the problem, one that may have been festering for a long time, by focusing their attention and using their best coping skills. As the storm clears, people will often see their partners in a different light, perhaps seeing positives in the person and in the partnership, positives that somehow eluded them before the storm.

For some, the damage will be so deep that reconciliation will never be an option. In that case people might take some comfort in knowing that the pain will eventually subside and statistically they will likely view themselves as "happier" a year after the separation. If reconciliation is judged to be possible, the proceedings are likely to be highly emotionally charged and the settlement will need to carefully consider the approach and timing.

It was once thought that it was best for offending partners to make a commitment to themselves to never repeat the adulterous behaviour and to keep the event a secret. Research now tells us that the second part is not so. It turns out that keeping infidelity a secret is actually more toxic to a marriage and that the marriage has a greater chance of surviving when the offending party reveals the affair first. It is a reality that over time, almost all dishonesty and deception is discovered and because it was not revealed in advance, the partner questions every aspect of the relationship, a situation that often leads to breakdown.

It is quite common for couples who are experiencing difficulties to confide in friends, sometimes with friends of the opposite gender - or same gender when they are bisexual or "bi-curious." The connection usually begins honestly through a friendship, but the sharing of relationship problems is frequently intimate and can easily lead to an extramarital "affair."

Many couples will experience the pain of an affair, resulting in strong emotions of anger, resentment, humiliation and retaliation, commonly resulting in a separation. It doesn't have to be so. If infidelity has occurred in your relationship don't be pushed by others or by emotion into calling for an immediate separation. Infidelity will destroy trust, security and intimacy and grieving that loss is natural and to be expected. Allow time to mentally process the adultery, to express feelings and to grieve the loss of trust. Then work must begin to demonstrate true remorse and to understand the root cause.

More and more couples are finding that if they work on saving the partnership, the relationship grows beyond what it was previously. However, the work is difficult and will require sacrifices and compromises from both sides, but reconciliation is possible if both parties are unwavering and agree to a specific process, preferably involving a professional therapist.

CHAPTER 18:
COMMUNICATION

"I have been in relationships in the past where communication wasn't great, and when it is, it makes it so much easier to talk to each other."

Hannah Bronfmann

There have been many surveys and studies that ask the question: "What was the cause of your divorce?" There are of course many answers from sexual incompatibility to different interests and expectations to lack of commitment, but the most frequent responses identified money, infidelity and one other. The biggest destroyer of relationships is poor communication.

Communication can be defined as the "exchanging of the meaning of information." But it's not that simple, because communication has both visible and invisible parts. In fact, it is a very complex process that is essential to the success of every relationship and every organization in our world. Academics will profess that there are several models of communication with several components to each. One of the most frequently taught model is illustrative of the complexity of the process. It describes the sender and receiver with their varied personalities, values and biases, the medium that carries the message, the context in which the message was sent, the message itself and the feedback about that message. Within those six parts there lies a myriad of possible failures.

Following is a typical communication scenario. A young couple arrives home from work together. She is tired and wants a few minutes to relax and he is hungry. Oblivious to her needs, he asks, "What's for dinner." She hears, "Why isn't dinner ready?" Her fatigue from the day's events changed the meaning of his message and she retorts, "I'm tired, find your own dinner for a change." Now the invisible communication in tone, body language and an inference that he doesn't do his share of meal preparation dominates the exchange. To fuel matters, he has never shared a feeling with her that he thinks she doesn't do her share of the home chores and her comment is heard as particularly unfair. "Fine, I'll do just that!" he exclaims, as he leaves the exchange in anger. A simple question has become a significant source of conflict that probably influenced the relationship for the remainder of the day, or longer.

So why is it that when we live with a person that we care for deeply, we can so readily slip into an exchange that breeds anger and derision? The answer to that may be as simple as poor communication skills. Or of course it can be more serious, such as in what is viewed as "the child" of dysfunctional communication - contempt. Examples of contempt are contained in what men tend to cite as the top communication problem in their relationship - nagging and complaining. Women's top complaint is that their spouse doesn't validate their opinions or feelings. Discounting, nagging and complaining, all come from a position of superiority, leaving the receiver of the message with feelings of being disrespected and disliked.

The other major factors that contribute to dysfunctional communication are criticism of the other person's personality, defensiveness and isolation - which is essentially a refusal to engage in communication. Criticism can be a useful part of any relationship, if it is well intentioned and done with tact. There are complaints in every relationship, but when they are presented as a defect in the other person's personality or character, the response is not likely to be receptive. Defensiveness is another problem, but if understood, is really just a method of warding off a perceived attack. Unfortunately, when we are defending ourselves, it is unlikely our partners view will be listened to. Instead, we are likely to respond with excuses or righteous indignation, often in the form of a counter attack. Isolation, or a refusal to engage the partner in conversation prevents any possibility of a resolution to a disagreement or conflict. Men appear to be more prone to isolation and often times they even see it as a positive characteristic. "We never fight," they will boast.

So, if we deal with the anger behind feelings of contempt and we improve our communication skills, is that all we require to do in order to improve our relationships and avoid separation? In fact, sometimes it is, along with a strong commitment to making things work. In one study almost half of the divorced individuals admitted that they wished they or their ex-spouse had tried harder to work through their differences. Interestingly the results indicated that although both parties were perceived to be at fault, most of the respondents thought they had tried harder than their mates. Thirty-one percent of the men wished that they had worked harder, but seventy-four percent said they wished their wives had worked harder. The women had similar views with thirteen percent of the women wishing they had worked harder, but sixty-five percent said they wished their ex-husbands had worked harder to save the relationship. The other half of the people in the study had no interest whatsoever in a reconciliation and sometimes for good reason.

There are obviously times when a separation is best for everyone involved, particularly when there is no willingness to get help or to make adjustments. Examples might be when there is an addiction or severe mental illness, where the partner is overly controlling, when there is repeated adultery and obviously when there is abuse of the spouse or of children. Of course, there may also just be the reality that the differences are so great so as to be irreconcilable.

In most situations, the motivation for separation begins early in the relationship and comes directly from something as simple - or as complex - as poor communication. The solution then is to improve the way we relate. And that doesn't mean just agreeing with each other. What it does mean is honest and open conversations about issues and then an effort to work towards a resolution. Seems easy enough, so why do so many couples have trouble getting there? The first reason is that they have no ground rules for arguments. It is important that through a disagreement people still feel respected and valued, so the ground rules need to contain things like no yelling and no personal attacks.

A second reason communication can fail is that people don't realize that it is usually the second response in a conversation that determines where it goes. A response can easily diffuse or accelerate a stressful situation as in the example of the young couple's exchange after arriving home from work. If her response to his question had been "I'm exhausted honey, can you give me a few minutes or find something yourself tonight," rather than "I'm tired, get your own dinner for a change," it is very unlikely that the reminder of that hostile and escalating conversation would have occurred.

A third reason for communication breakdown is the failure to convey affection and intimacy along with the words we use. Communication has a silent part that is so very powerful. It is difficult to fight if you are hearing kind words and feeling the energy of a warm touch. This must of course occur before a situation escalates into an argument.

The fourth reason for communication problems is a failure to listen carefully. Listening means really hearing what someone's saying and then doing our best to understand their point of view. Body language that might convey distraction, boredom or pre-occupation will leave a much different message than the "active listening" we should be engaged in. You can't respond to "you never listen to me!" with, "that's a strange way to start a conversation."

Yelling! The fifth reason for communication failure is in some minds, the first and most important reason. When we feel angry it is natural to start raising our voices in an effort to relieve our tension and win the argument, although it often causes more trouble than not. It is natural to feel emotion and the raising of voices is natural, but there is a line where respect becomes lost. Yelling unleashes strong, negative energy and those feelings weaken the spoken word, resulting in defensiveness, more anger and retaliation. If we don't temper our reactions, we will cut off communication.

The sixth reason for poor communication is closely connected with yelling and that is the failure to respect a partner's position. Whether one agrees with another or not, there is no value in conveying disrespect. It is too easy to focus on our own needs without being sensitive to those of a partner. When in a disagreement, if we can "stand back" and try to suppress our own feelings temporarily in favor of trying to understand a partner, the action will go a long way towards a resolution to the matter. Looking at any situation from a different vantage point, for example, placing ourselves "in other people's shoes" can allow us to see how our own behavior might not be helpful.

Failure number seven is with respect to timing. Bringing up important issues at an inopportune time can easily result in a negative response. When people are busy, in a rush, tired, distracted or hungry, forcing a serious conversation - unless it is essential to do so - rarely brings about a resolution. We may not of course always be aware that our timing is wrong, but as that becomes evident, the appropriate choice of words can easily defer a matter to a later date while avoiding an escalation of tensions.

It may take some practice to change old communication approaches, however we will find it quite amazing as to how the energy between partners can change in a very short time with sensitive, thoughtful and intentional communication. The idea that great relationships require hard work may conflict with the romantic belief that true love is all we need, but even the most loving connections can become distant.

So, assess your communication skills along with those of your partner. Are there uncontrolled emotions? Does one of you consistently just leave the discussion? Is there a competitive attitude or need to be right or to win? Who is the judge, as in expressing thoughts and feelings with blame and criticism? Finally, is there selfishness, a focus on "me" rather than "we."

Try working with your partner on a communication agreement that includes ground rules for dealing with differences. Rules such as using words of respect, no personal attacks, restrained emotions, moderate voice levels, staying put, attentive listening, questions of clarification and appropriate timing. It is also wise to set time aside daily for uninterrupted conversations about experiences, aspirations, satisfactions, gratefulness, goals, frustrations and feelings.

With proper care and nurturing it is possible to create the partnership we all so desire. The key has to do with recognizing the need and being willing to work at it. Otherwise, it is probably time to move on.

CHAPTER 19: ADDICTION

"Relationships are worth fighting for, but you just can't be the only one fighting."
                    The love Bits

The power of addictive drugs is not and will probably never be understood by people who "have not been there." The following is an excerpt from the book Addicts in Wonderland. *"The pipe was a small brass plumbing fitting on the top of a baby food jar, with about a foot of clear plastic tubing attached to a second hole in the tin top. The young disheveled woman placed a small piece of crack cocaine in the brass head and melted it. She then took my money and instructed me to suck slowly and inhale the smoke deep into my lungs. I glanced around the park and then up and down the street to ensure that there were no police. I then inhaled slowly on the plastic tubing. I could see puffy white smoke fill the tiny jar and then curl up the tube until it reached my mouth. I then drew it in to my lungs slowly and methodically. "Ok, now hold it for a few seconds and exhale," the woman further instructed. The effect was immediate; from the lungs to the brain in seconds. I was completely unprepared for the intensity of the feeling. It was indescribable, a euphoria I had never before experienced. I was completely in that moment. No history, no future, no tension, no pain, no fear. "Are you ok?" asked the woman's friend as I stumbled back to a street bench, salivated and stared into space. I never thought it possible, but I was hooked on that first "blast." I became an instant addict, craving that intense feeling that cascaded through every organ and gland in my body; launching a craving that would simply not stop."*

That experience may sound enticing, but one needs to understand the whole picture. Again, a quote from the book Addicts in Wonderland. *"I now really believed that I was at my ``bottom." I believed that, because for the first time, I began to realize that there was no bottom. Addiction was an abyss and there was always a deeper and darker place to go."* The drug high is fleeting, is never enough and always leads to chaos, dysfunction, collapsed relationships and more often than not, death. While cocaine doesn't seize everyone this quickly, the right substance or experience can in fact have the effect of taking control of the individual immediately. It will usually occur over time, but when it does, the consequences are immense.

Addiction can be defined as a chronic, relapsing brain disease characterized by compulsive drug or experience seeking, despite any harmful consequences. Synonyms, or words that mean the same as addiction are compulsion, craving, obsession and dependence. Whatever the addiction, it becomes a craving that will simply not stop. In its simplest form that is the essence of addiction, an inability to stop.

So what are the most common addictions and how do we tell if a person is becoming addicted? In both the U.S. and Canada, the greatest use of a drug is with caffeine. One hundred milligrams a day can cause a level of dependence, however the conventional wisdom is that caffeine does not qualify as an "addictive" substance. The product then with the greatest addictive potential in terms of numbers is tobacco. There are an estimated 40 million individuals with a tobacco addiction, more than double the number of people who are addicted to alcohol. About a quarter of the alcohol addiction number of almost 20 million people are addicted to cannabis, followed by some 2 million people with addictions to painkillers like Vicoden, Codein and Oxycontin. There are a million cocaine users, a half million heroin users and another half million prescription drug users of Xanax, Valium, Ritalin, Lunesta and numerous other stimulating and sedating products. And there seem to be new street "designer" drugs every day - often laced with the killer drug Fentanyl - where even the smallest amounts are lethal. Collectively, they create untold havoc in relationships right across the two nations.

In addition to drugs, an unknown number of North Americans - estimated in the millions - are addicted to gambling, sex, pornography, the Internet, video games, shopping and even work. They can't seem to control these compulsions and the relationship consequences are usually not pretty. There are many theories about how to tell if your interests and likes, or those of a partner, have become addictions, but the dependency is pretty obvious if we are not living in denial. Simply put, the addiction will invariably result in dysfunctional behaviors - excessive spending, risk taking, dishonesty, secretiveness, neglected health, problems at work or school, changes in usual conducts and of course an inability to control the activity or consumption.

Beyond observing these behaviors, it is possible to assess if one has an addiction by completing a four-question test called the "CAGE," its name derived from an acronym for its four questions. The unassuming test has been evaluated extensively and in spite of its simplicity has a "sensitivity" or accuracy rate of ninety-three percent for identifying excessive use and a ninety-one percent sensitivity for identifying addiction. The test is now being used routinely by physicians during annual physical examinations, or in a specific assessment of alcoholism. It can also be useful as a self-evaluation tool in many other addictions by simply substituting a word or words for one's own particular obsession (i.e.) using cocaine, for the word "drinking." Two "yes" responses to the following questions are considered indicative of a problem.

1. Have you ever felt you needed to **C**ut down on your drinking?
2. Have people **A**nnoyed you by criticizing your drinking?

3. Have you ever felt **G**uilty about drinking?
4. Have you ever felt you needed a drink first thing in the morning (**E**ye-opener)

As you can see from this simple questionnaire, the issue of control, or "an inability to stop" is central to an addiction. This inability to control oneself occurs because in the "normal" brain, the "reward circuits" respond to pleasurable experiences by releasing the neurotransmitter dopamine. The chemical creates feelings of pleasure and tells the brain that this experience is something important, to pay attention and remember it. Addictions hijack this system, causing unusually large amounts of dopamine to flood the body. This excess of dopamine is what causes the "high" or euphoria as described earlier by the cocaine user.

The brain then adapts in response to the overwhelming surges in dopamine by decreasing the number of dopamine receptors available, thus diminishing the function of the reward circuit. These changes in brain function create lasting memories that link the addictive experience to a pleasurable reward and over time this memory is conditioned to become stronger and stronger. Addicts feel compelled to drink more alcohol, use more drugs, watch more pornography or to increase whatever substance or behavior they are addicted to in order to bring their dopamine levels up, therefore requiring ever larger amounts to achieve the initial dopamine high. This increasing demand is known as tolerance.

How do we develop addictions in the first place? Addiction specialists will tell you that these cravings can occur genetically; that the cellular demand for a substance is carried inter-generationally. This genetic transfer can occur within families or groups. For example, we often see it with grandfather, father and son. It is also now believed by some researches that both aboriginal North Americans and the Irish have a genetic predisposition to alcohol addiction.

In other situations, the addiction is learned through "identification" or "modeling." Many people repeat the addictions of their parents or they unwittingly develop a different addiction and repeat the nature of the relationship their parents experienced. How many daughters of men with alcoholism marry another man with the same problem? In a third form of addiction the internal scales become tipped after a lengthy period of substance or experience misuse and the behavior cannot be stopped without help.

This inability to stop is often accompanied by a second virtually universal characteristic of addiction and that is the inability to maintain a relationship. With the possible exception of tobacco and work addiction, or perhaps in situations where both members in a relationship are addicted, no duo can successfully survive an active addiction without help.

No one. Some people would argue that cannabis should be considered an exception as well, because like tobacco and work addiction they believe it does not contribute to relationship problems. That may or may not be true, but recent studies do show it can be both addictive and dangerous. Those studies are providing pretty clear evidence that the current much stronger forms of the drug are causing brain structure changes affecting judgment, comprehension, memory, motivation and perception, with the possibility of psychosis in heavy chronic users. Not to mention lung disease. Several States and more recently Canada, have legalized the use of Cannabis for recreational purposes, with reports of both positive and negative results. What is most dangerous will be any perception that the drug is not dangerous. As with all drugs, misuse will have dire consequences. And if smoked, users should realize that both first and second hand smoke are more carcinogenic that tobacco, and that product kills 443,000 Americans and 37,000 Canadians every year.

While people with addictions marry at the same rate as the general public, it is also true that people with addictions divorce at a rate much higher than couples that do not have dependencies. Statistically, almost none of these relationships survive. It could be argued then, that one of the ways we might reduce the rate of relationship separations would be by avoiding people who suffer with addictions. In reality, even when an addiction exists, most people involved in an intimate relationship don't recognize it, live in denial about it, or believe they can fix it. In other situations, the activity or substance misuse develops after the couple begin living together.

Living with someone can be challenging enough with the daily need to put another person's needs alongside your own and while doing so, make life-changing decisions together. That takes a great deal of energy, commitment and compromise. When substance misuse begins to take a toll on the user's psychological health, their partners will see them as very different people. The need for a "fix" will always take precedence over the needs of the partner or the needs of the family if one exists.

It is also a truism that substance misuse and alcoholism are closely associated with aggression and violence. It is common for the spouse, usually the woman, to be subjected to humiliation, abuse and harassment, sometimes for years before finally deciding to take action and pursue a separation. And in many situations abusive and dependent relationships can be extraordinarily difficult to extricate oneself from, a reality verified by the large number of women who year after year obtain legal restraining orders and police protection, yet are still assaulted and even murdered by an angry or jealous ex-friend or ex-husband "high" or intoxicated on one drug or another. Whenever the onset, whether before or after people move in together, or whatever the behaviors, addiction is probably the most destructive force a relationship will experience and any union is most certainly doomed to fail unless both the addicted individual and the partner get help for their problems.

But what kind of help is available? Science has made only modest progress in the treatment of addictions, with only a few significant innovations in the past seventy years. Family interventions are relatively new and there are some new drugs that help diminish the cravings for some opioids. There are also recent medications to decrease cravings or provide a substitute for tobacco and alcohol, counseling approaches have improved and there is a range of therapeutic approaches used by psychologists for behavioral change and skill development.

Some residential treatment centers now focus on "harm reduction" rather than "abstinence," however, the prevailing approach to treatment used almost everywhere was developed by the *Hazelton Institute* in Minnesota. It is a strategy based on the 12 Step philosophy of Alcoholics Anonymous, released in 1939. The 12-step approach dominates the recovery industry in counseling programs, treatment centers and of course in community support strategies. Unfortunately, the retention rate from these programs is very low. Alcoholics Anonymous itself acknowledges that almost a third of the people who attend AA leave within the first month and that number increases to over half after three months.

Others don't attend at all because the program contains methods or theories that they disagree with. The AA partner program Al-anon developed for families provides for family information and support and it is generally highly regarded by participants. However, it is frequently frustrating for partners who get involved with Al-anon and then find that their spouse or partner abandoned AA or another of the "anonymous" groups.

Notwithstanding the limitations, the AA program seems to have worked for millions over the past eight decades. With over two million members in 150 countries world-wide, there are obviously those that find the program helpful. In summary, the 12 Step approach requires the participant to admit they can't control their addiction without help. They must then recognize that there are greater powers that can and will help them. Then they examine past problems focusing on strengths and limitations and they make restitution to the people they have harmed. They must then learn to live a new life connected to some external power and help others that still suffer.

So if relationships cannot survive within most active addictions and if the Anonymous programs are the "only game in town," it is important to understand why AA doesn't work for many people. It is perhaps even more important to see how the program might be adapted. The "Anonymous" programs basic tenants are good and the major reasons that people leave are three-fold. First, because they don't believe in a God and in particular the Christian God, secondly because they disagree that they are "powerless" and need to "turn things over," and finally, because people are encouraged to "live the program" and to re-visit their issues and problems over and over, sometimes for years. In spite of these perceived deficiencies the steps can still work with modifications. For example, you can substitute for the word "God" with something else more important than your finite self. That might take the form of life energy, or life source, or the universe, or a passion like writing or art, or even in helping others.

As for the concept of powerlessness, you can view it as being over some things, but not over defeating the disease. The truth is we are rarely powerless over how we respond to how life's events affect us. For example, sailors may be powerless over the weather, but they are not powerless over learning to sail a stormy sea. Finally, you can visit issues once or twice and then move on. View yourself as in "recovery" rather than "addicted" or "alcoholic." If it is true that we attract to our life whatever we give our attention and energy to, (review chapter eight on energy) then the approach of starting a meeting by saying ""Hello, I am ___ I am an alcoholic," may attract more of that addiction.

In conclusion, a relationship with a person with an addiction can only survive if the addiction is in remission. Addictions are the leading cause of divorce before the age of 30 and there is often a connection to domestic violence and financial problems. While the experience of addiction can become a positive life-altering event for some, in reality it is not for most and those people in relationships with someone with an addiction need to realize that. Active addictions will make the responsibilities of a relationship almost impossible to handle for both the addicted individual and their partner. But experience has shown that even when circumstances seem hopeless in a relationship damaged by addiction, there is frequently hope for recovery. Setting boundaries is vital, as is showing patience, love, and support. Specific communication strategies, professional resources and modifications to the AA approach can all help.

Recognizing an addiction problem early in a relationship can sometimes be difficult because addictive personalities are often quite skilled at hiding their inclinations. Conversely, what may seem like an addiction may be youthful curiosity, experimentation or a response to some specific stressful life challenge. But addiction can be chronic and in fact usually does get worse over time. No matter the type of addiction, it is important to recognize warning signs and to seek help at an early stage, or to move on to a different relationship.

If you or your partner have an addiction or even think you may have a problem, honestly assess your ability to stop the use of a substance or activity. Examine your life in terms of your compulsion to do things, spend excessively, take risks, be secretive and deceitful, neglect health or experience problems with work, school or the police. Ask yourself the "CAGE" questions regarding Cutting down, feeling Annoyed, feeling Guilt and needing an early morning hit. (Eye opener).

A successful relationship will require dedication, responsibility, compromise, intimacy and trust. In contrast, an individual with an active addiction will place the addictive substance or activity above everything else and can meet none of the requirements. The nature of addiction is such that trust is difficult as the person will often lie, cheat and steal in order to feed their obsession. While showing love and support is vital for any partner, so is the setting of boundaries. Limits like determining what behaviors are acceptable and which are not and what the consequences are for violating them. A consistent response without "softening" and accepting no excuses is vital. Be prepared for numerous violations and frequent separations. If you set no boundaries you become an "enabler," a part of the problem and at risk yourself.

Addiction treatment programs work well for some and not for others. Although addiction is indeed a disease, if there is no motivation to get well, the chances of recovery are poor, whatever the treatment. It's kind of like receiving heart by-pass surgery while continuing to smoke, eat poorly and live in a stressful environment; the chances of recovery are modest at best.

Depending on the size of a community, local treatment resources may be available from interventionists, psychiatrists, psychologists, Alcoholics/Narcotics/Cocaine Anonymous groups, Al-anon groups, rehabilitation centers, hostels and a myriad of other resources. Costs will vary. In Canada, the government pays for most medical services. In the United States a range of private and government medical plans are available to some people through employers, brokers and private foundations. Alcoholics Anonymous is available almost everywhere and there is no charge.

Partners can be abused, disappointed, lied to, stolen from, dishonored and yet they stay. The usual reason is fear. They are afraid of what might happen to their partner, they are afraid of loneliness, they are afraid of how their family might respond, they are afraid of moving, that are afraid of their finances. The list goes on, so they stay. There is no value in staying in an addictive relationship that leads to the loving partner becoming ill as well.

Maintaining a relationship within an addiction can be spirit and life destroying. Is it "till death do us part?" When do you give in and move on? If you have tried every measure from intervention to rehabilitation and the addiction and chaos continue, it is probably wise to face your fears, consult a lawyer and protect yourself. Although your decision is ultimately individual, making it with family, friends or a professional is often essential to dealing with the accompanying fear. It may also be essential to staying alive.

CHAPTER 20: ILLNESS

"Never give up on a person with an illness. When "i" becomes "we," illness becomes wellness."
                                                    Shannon Alder

Several studies have found quite varied yet startling results, reporting that from 30 to 75 percent of relationships that are plagued by chronic illness end in separation. The wide-ranging results probably reflect what diseases are included in the definition of "chronic." By using government statistics, half of all North Americans live with a chronic condition like cancer, diabetes, heart disease, chronic fatigue syndrome, Lupus, Crohn's disease and others. It is important to note however, that this statistic is a bit suspect because the "half of all Americans" number also includes less serious chronic conditions like asthma, arthritis, anemia, oral herpes and so on. Nonetheless, no matter how we view the numbers – thirty or seventy-five percent - there is no disputing that chronic illnesses are a major contributor to relationship disruption and dissolution.

Individuals who are beginning a relationship sometimes wonder if they should continue at all, while longer term partnered couples may think they are unable to cope any more. In most situations the sick individual will fight feelings of guilt and inadequacy, while the healthier partner may feel angry and victimized, thinking, "this is more than I bargained for." At the beginning of a relationships a debilitating chronic illnesses can make dating particularly difficult with one of the most significant concerns being the issue of "disclosure." If one reads dating web sites and blogs, the question of when to share the information about an illness with a prospective partner is the most common apprehension. Sharing too soon could scare the person off and sharing too late might lead to a lack of trust. Some choose to be upfront from the beginning while others wait until the consideration of exclusive dating. Disclosure becomes even more important if the chronic illness is transmissible. For example, early disclosure is critical in the case of diseases like AIDS, hepatitis and other highly contagious diseases.

Once there has been an admission and a couple chooses to continue a relationship, it is still important for them to realize that only one hurdle has been crossed and more await. There are very few things in a relationship, other than money, communication, adultery and addiction, that test relationships like a chronic illness does. Yet most people underestimate the difficulties a chronic condition creates. In fact, most people don't even consider the possibility. Denial from "being in love" prevents them from even thinking about the potential of a life changing illness. They probably eliminated the phrase from their marriage vows or breezed through the "in sickness and in health" clause without much thought. If they had thought about it at all, they probably pictured the intent of the phrase as meaning they might have to serve their partner chicken soup or run to the pharmacy for painkillers or an antibiotic.

A major calamity is rarely part of the picture that people see in their future and it is certainly not a consideration when planning a wedding, a "move-in" or a honeymoon. All relationships face obstacles, but most of them just aren't as pervasive as with a chronic illness that usually remain with the couple 24/7. Imagine the feelings in the following real life examples. Kevin is a very active fun loving man and his partner is constantly fatigued and just wants to stay home. Nicole quits a career job that she loves, to stay home and care for a husband who has Lou Gering's Disease. Ann has cancer and asks her husband not to be a "martyr" and remain at home with her, giving up his interests and hobbies. Gordon does little else but drive to the hospital each day in order to spend time with his partner with Alzheimers. There are millions of stories of loyalty, dedication, commitment and sacrifice where partners are required to fill the roles of spouse, caretaker and nurse, and the challenge is especially great in the case of some mental health conditions like Alzheimer's disease. Sometimes too great.

If a disease is diagnosed later in a relationship, a partner may conclude "that was not part of the deal" and they may wish not to make the necessary sacrifices. On the other side of that coin, it is not uncommon for a chronically ill person to not want to subject a partner, or anyone else for that matter, to the consequences of their disease, the potentially debilitating symptoms and in many situations the psychological depression that follows. This is particularly so in the case of major illnesses like cancer, heart disease, lung disease, stroke or a mental illness like dementia, severe anxiety or a depressive condition.

While women initiate most divorces and separations, the decision to exit a relationship where illness is a factor tends to be more likely with men. Women seem more inclined to be loyal and to accept the need to be a caregiver. When a partner is diagnosed with a chronic illness, the realization that life may never again be the same seeps in slowly. More often than not, the existence of the illness materialized out of nowhere. Initially the individual, whether it is the ill person or the family member, is inclined to privately deny the diagnosis; "there must be a mistake." When the reality does set in, it is quite likely that anger will dominate the feelings. If that anger is expressed in a healthy manner, the couple is likely to move on. Unfortunately, that progress is often after both parties experience a deep depression. In most situations, through appropriate strategies and support, the health condition will eventually be accepted and work can begin on dealing with the future.

The extent to which that future will be dealt with as a couple or with one party leaving the relationship will be highly influenced by at least five factors; the severity and prognosis of the ailing spouse's illness, the amount of outside support they have, the degree to which old social connections are maintained, the personal traits of the individuals - like how well they deal with distress, and of course their previous satisfaction with the union. Age is also a factor with illness driven separations most often occurring between ages 51 and 61, where in recent years many people have begun expressing dissatisfaction with their relationship anyway.

In some reported cases a separation has even been precipitated by the lack of satisfaction with the kind of care the ill person was receiving. Women seemed more inclined to be unhappy with the care they got, while men tended to be more uncomfortable with the care they gave. In some cases, this factor alone resulted in the relationship being terminated. It seems that many women preferred being looked after by friends, family members and hired help when they judged that their partner wasn't up to the task.

Overlaying all of these issues is the contemporary attitude about an "ethic of obligation to others, toward an obligation to self" - a kind of entitlement to the good life. That attitude, while prevalent in today's middle age and growing old population, is of course not what a chronically ill person wants to hear or experience. One's fantasy would be that if we were to have a debilitating condition or if our life appeared as though it might be cut short, we would want our partner by our side. We would want to believe that any individual that we had trusted would be emotionally strong enough, loyal enough and loving enough to stick by "till death do us part."

Unfortunately, even the best of relationships will be strained within the marriage vow of "in sickness and in health," but there are a few strategies that can help. The first rule in dealing with a chronic illness, as in most relationship issues, is to communicate. Talking openly about challenges will lead to problem solving, and a feeling of intimacy will be a by-product of the teamwork. But don't be consumed with talking about the illness; visit a problem, find a solution and move on, or you may invite more of the same.

If you are dealing with a chronic illness, depression is normal, as is the need for more information and the need to express some thoughts and feelings that may not be helpful when they are expressed "bed-side." There are options to giving up, but they won't seem evident if you are not honest and clear about your specific needs. Watch for signs of distress, re-negotiate responsibilities and tasks around the home and arrange "time-away" and respite for both partners. A chronic illness can dissolve a relationship, but it can also strengthen it. The outcome will be determined not by the severity of the illness, but by the commitment to and the strength of the solving effort.

Are you talking openly? Do you have assistance? Do you have opportunities for respite? Are you maintaining or even strengthening your social connections? Have you considered counselling? Professionals and people who have had similar experiences and understanding can be incredibly helpful.

CHAPTER 21: AGING

"My wife and I were happy for twenty years. And then we met.

     Rodney Dangerfield

The rate of divorce for couples over age 50 has increased so much in recent years that it has prompted new "buzzwords." Grey divorce. While the statistics regarding divorce rates in North America are declining as young people opt for "common-law" relationships, people over 55 are divorcing in greater numbers. This increasing divorce rate among "seniors" is relatively new, having taken a dramatic jump over the last two decades. And the majority of those entering new relationships are not re-marrying either, perhaps because some of those divorces are initiated by people well into their 70's. In 1990, fewer than 10 percent of divorces were people over 55, but over the past twenty-five years the number has leaped to one-in-four or 25 percent. Why are "seniors" separating? There are probably as many reasons as there are people, but an over-arching explanation may be that at an age where people think there will be peace, solitude and relaxation, they find their lives to be boring and mundane or alternatively, chaotic and stressful.

One stress factor is retirement. Retired couples often face difficulty in adjusting to a life together that doesn't include work. People who once defined themselves by what they did, will often experience an identity crisis. Who are they without their profession and title? Meanwhile, spouses accustomed to being alone most of the day must adjust to having somebody else around. Or in some cases people who have enjoyed relatively independent lives with intense career experiences find they are now with the same person 24/7, while other relationships and contacts are largely severed. No matter how much they care, too much exclusive time together in any relationship can foster a range of negative emotions. Even really "good" marriages can have difficulty with the retirement transition and "bad marriages" may not survive. Statistically if one or both of the spouses experienced divorce in the past, they are even more at risk of divorce later in life. The divorce rate for second relationships jumps by 10 percent and by more than an additional 10 percent for a third.

A second factor that might explain later life separation is simply the reality of change. As we age it is not uncommon for two people who have lived quite independently, to lose touch with who their partner really is. We all change over our lifetime and as that happens we may change into people that our spouses don't like. In other cases, the individual never really was the kind of person the spouse had hoped for. Anger, frustration and disappointment may have for years been "swept under the rug," or simply lived with for whatever reason.

A third reason can surface when retirement plans differ or when the disparities between two couples become more prominent. For example, if the husband is driven to continue working while the wife retires and looks forward to travel and a more peaceful life. He will then feel pressured and she will invariably be aimless, lonely and resentful.

The so-called "empty-nest" syndrome is a fourth factor. As children reach adulthood and leave home, one or both parents may feel they are no longer needed in life. Marriages that remain intact "for the children" are particularly at risk at this time, because the reason for the marriage may appear to no longer exist. For some people -often couples who have children at a young age - life was a whirl-wind of career, child demands and the unrelenting pressures of living in contemporary society, resulting in a propensity to look "outside" at the world. They probably never really contemplated who they were, and then in later life began to feel a need to look "inside" in order to "find themselves."

Surprisingly to some, infidelity is a common factor in senior divorce. The sex drive in older people will diminish at different rates and there is sometimes a temptation - particularly with men - to satisfy that urge when an opportunity presents itself. And opportunities abound in North America with millions of widows and divorcees living alone in every part of Canada and the United States. So much so, that another buzzword "cougar" has emerged to describe middle-aged or older women who prey on "desirable men." While the term most frequently refers to older women and younger men, the senior with financial resources, a professional history and "class," is a favored target for seduction.

Another factor is health. There is a saying that in marriage that a women is a mistress in youth, a domestic in mid-life and a nurse in old age. There may well be some truth to that, as men tend to be older in most relationships and are likely to be less healthy than their partners. Statistically men will become infirm (and die) before their partner. Even after a lifetime together, it can be a difficult thing to live with someone who is in constant need, and some spouses do decide, "enough is enough."

The loss of stigma is another reason older people divorce. In the past, people in society and particularly in religious circles looked with disdain at a divorcing couple. In many communities, that is no longer the case. Freed from rejection by others, it becomes much easier (well, perhaps not "much" easier) to contemplate a separation. Women are now also more independent and empowered and much better equipped to act on their own from both psychological and financial perspectives.

Longevity is another reason. In the past, a 65 year-old might contemplate the few remaining years together and conclude that moving on just wasn't worth the effort. With an average life expectancy of 80 for women and 77 for men in the U.S. and 85 for women and 83 for men in Canada, seniors can now easily envision 20 more active years and they don't want them to be boring, loveless, lacking intimacy or full of tension and disappointment. For many, old age includes the pursuit of "peace," and people don't want to wait for that to be achieved along with an inscription on their gravestone.

Whatever the reasons, most seniors who contemplate separating will do so with great difficulty. Yet many of them don't seem to carefully consider all of the consequences. And there are many. Family disruption, estrangement from children, selling property, dividing assets, financial strain, loneliness, experiencing the anger of people who are important to them, chaos in their lives and moving homes to name a few. Divorce and separation are not unlike losing a spouse through death and deep grieving is a common experience. And like the prolonged death of an ill partner, the passing of a mate may come with great relief. However, it is then common to feel guilty about feeling that relief.

At a minimum, if a separation is being considered, all of the consequences should be well measured and understood, along with a plan of action to address those consequences. Before proceeding though, a kind of "sabbatical" where the parties live separately for a while can be very helpful. An unhappy partner may also wish to re-visit their youth and contemplate their life experience in relation to the dream they once had. The professional help of a counselor and if necessary, a lawyer can be invaluable. There is for example, an alternative to a decree of divorce if there are no children involved. A simple "Separation Agreement" provides the details of the separation and of reconciliation, if that should be desired in the future. That agreement should detail that no legal divorce is contemplated at this time, but that the "Parties" agree to live separately without disturbance, to disclose assets, to agree on maintenance, the payment of debts, asset distribution and on a method of reconciliation if later desired.

Regardless of our efforts to really know someone, there will always be surprises, shifts and changes. Through much of life, the demands of family, career and accumulating wealth dominate our time and it is all too common that people grow apart slowly without even realizing it. The challenge of any intimate relationship is maintaining the love and respect for your partner. An individual that you need to know - over and over and over.

A loving relationship is an organic entity and as such it will either grow or die. In order to flourish it must receive nourishment regularly. Unfortunately, relationships for many people are about their own personal happiness; about "me." The reality is that when people make things about "me," they aren't. The desire for self-fulfillment and happiness are legitimate and worthy goals, but what about personal growth and learning? Happiness, like any other desire is not something that simply comes to us, but rather is primarily a function of our relationship with others. If we talk to people on their "death beds" they will invariably tell us that their satisfaction in life came from the love and service of others, rarely if ever from selfish pursuits.

Many people find it difficult to see themselves as elderly. They speak of the "old people" down the block who are their age. They see their parents in the mirror, but quickly look away. The think their spouse is aging more quickly than they are. If they faced their reality they would see that none of their contemporaries look like they once did, or that their fantasy about a new young partner includes the reality of divorce chaos, new relationship challenges and the rigors of a relationship where the age differences are large.

Are you able to see what you saw when you got married? Do you understand the biology of aging, the reality that hormones and chemicals are different, as are some of our behaviors? Do you deal with feelings and issues as they arise and make your partners needs as important as your own? Do you make a daily decision to invest in relationship growth by finding time for intimacy and meaningful conversation? Do you spend some time apart, pursuing personal interests or visiting friends? Do you have fun? Is it possible to stay connected or re-connect to what should and could be the most important relationship in your life?

SECTION 5: *Together or Apart*

CHAPTER 22: BEDLAM

Losing a mate to death is devastating, but it's not a personal attack like divorce. When somebody you love stops loving you and walks away, it's an insult beyond comparison."

Sue Merrel

The word Bedlam was the notorious name of the 17th century British mental asylum of St. Mary Bethlehem, the first known such facility in the world. The word came to mean "uproar and confusion" and it continues to this day to be used to describe chaos and madness. Rather like divorce and separation.

When we read the statistics we know that the matter of relationship dissolution is pandemic in North America. To review a few numbers, while India has a one percent divorce to marriage ratio" the U.S. is closer to 53 percent and Canada is at 48 percent. Only a few countries have higher rates, with Sweden at the top at 55 percent. So why are so many people separating? The top three reasons have already been detailed;

stress over finances, poor communication and infidelity. The average marriage lasts between seven and eight years, with the participants becoming single again at around age thirty. Only one-third of all couples will celebrate their 25th anniversary, although that may change as some studies report the numbers of divorces in same sex relationships is only half of that of the "straight" public. Then when people stay together, surveys say that only one third of them say they consider themselves "happy."

For most, the collapse of an intimate relationship is an extremely painful experience. Some people have temporary setbacks, some suffer excruciating long term hurt and others find themselves on a debilitating downward spiral that never seems to end. An outcome that is not dis-similar to that experienced by soldiers and first responders who suffer Post Traumatic Stress Disorder (PTSD). Although most people only associate PTSD with battle-scarred soldiers and emergency responders, any overwhelming life experience can trigger the condition, particularly if the event was volatile and uncontrollable - a typical experience in divorce and separations. The symptoms of post-traumatic stress include upsetting memories, flashbacks, nightmares and feelings of distress and panic. Soldiers, first responders and newly divorced/separated alike report difficulty sleeping, loss of interest, depression, hopelessness, irritability, poor concentration and hyper-vigilance (constantly remaining on alert.) It is also common to feel regret, anger, guilt, poor self-esteem, identity doubts and distrust. Many people experience new aches and pains, develop dietary problems - either eating incessantly or not at all - and are prone to substance abuse, usually alcohol. Mostly though, they feel lonely. Lonely, lonely, lonely.

Children will also feel the effects of a separation. Although they are resilient and in most situations will recover, they may initially experience sleep problems, incontinence, intense fear, compulsive play, phobias, irritability, worry, aggression and destructive behavior.

The emotional response to separation is only one facet of the life changes that follow. There will be alterations in social and economic conditions and there are often financial challenges such as a move to more modest accommodation and additional work. There may also be more work at home and along with that extra work comes an inability to do many tasks that were part of a couple's "division of labor."

In many cases there are ongoing legal battles about child support and visitation. The relationships with the children often change, with parents becoming overly attentive or harsh and punitive without even realizing it. The children respond accordingly with numerous dysfunctional behaviors. Adolescents will often act out, getting into neighborhood, school or legal difficulty. As a rule, parental contact with children often drops away. Studies report that a working mother's time with her children is on average reduced from twenty-five to only five hours a week and the father's time is reduced from twenty to two hours. Then the majority of fathers virtually "disappear" from their child's life after the first year.

If new relationships develop in younger families, the challenges of "blended" family's surface. About 75 percent of the 1.2 million Americans who divorce each year will eventually enter a new relationship. Most of them have children and they soon find that "step-family" life is more complex than they had ever imagined. It is full of attachment difficulties, allegations of preferential treatment, busy schedules and squabbling step-siblings. Then there are the complicated feelings and communication challenges amongst both the new and old partners. People often fall in love (or perhaps lust) with people who are lots of fun to be with. Then as the relationship grows, they complain that they want this fun-loving person to "grow up." Growing up is about behaving responsibly, but it is also about insight and judgment. Insight tends to come from spending quiet time looking "inside" and judgment comes from many experiences with healthy feedback. Both features are as a rule in short supply when we are young. Failure to choose wisely in the first place is often a big part of having to look at failure in the relationship. If you didn't look carefully at both yourself and your potential partner –and most of us don't - you may need to look carefully at a divorce lawyer. But it is not hopeless. With the right approach you can achieve a life that is fulfilling and joyful, perhaps even better than it was originally.

In summary, there are four broad categories of consequence following a divorce action - the personal and emotional challenges, the social and relationship changes, the effect on children and the economic modifications. Are you prepared for loneliness, anxiety, depression, guilt, fear and anger? Are you prepared for a different social status and changes in your relationship with family and friends? If children are involved, are you prepared for depression, anger and acting out. Finally, are you prepared for changes in your income, the need to work, or work longer, the need to work harder at home, the need to learn new life skills and the possible need to change living conditions? These consequences are obviously very serious and sometimes tough to overcome. That fact should lead to the careful consideration of a renewed effort if reconciliation is at all possible. It should not however, lead to a decision to remain in an impossible situation because of fear of the future.

A professional can help with this process, but so can an honest response to a few simple questions. For example, how do you feel when your partner is away, is with you, or is just coming or leaving? In what way and how often do you fight? Do you have common aspirations and goals? Do you have similar philosophies about child rearing? What is your relationship with your birth families and friends? Do you have shared ideas about saving and spending? These and other questions can help you, and only you, decide if a relationship is salvageable.

Not wanting to paint an unduly negative picture of parting, it is perhaps important to note that many separation actions do have a positive outcome in the long run. As was noted earlier, one study concluded that one year after a divorce, 80 percent of men and 50 percent of women thought their lives were better. But you have to get there and that usually isn't easy.

CHAPTER 23: CHILDREN

"My parents' divorce left me with a lot of sadness and pain. Acting, and especially humor, was my way of dealing with all that."

Jennifer Aniston

Braydon's parents divorced when he was still a baby. While the separation was typically volatile in the beginning, the couple "worked things out" in order to best serve their children. When Braydon's parents met other people and entered into new relationships, the two families maintained contact and even vacationed together. A "care-giver" at an early age, Braydon confided in both his grandfather and his grade two teacher that he felt quite sorry for more than half of his class. "Those poor kids only have one mom and one dad," he lamented.

Unfortunately, Braydon is a minority child in terms of attitude, buffered in part by his birth parents' commitment to his well-being in spite of their separation and by his adoptive parents loving care. Most children of broken relationships are not so fortunate and since the mid 70's half of all North American children could expect their families to break up. Since 1974, more than one million children a year in North America have watched their parent's separate and while those split-ups are fueled by many things, they are sometimes powered by a change in parental attitudes that see a divorce or separation in terms of an obligation to self, rather than an obligation to others. Individual happiness has become the new standard by which a relationship is judged. The family, once the dominion of obligation and responsibility has become subordinate to exploring personal happiness and the "potential of self." A related assumption is that the children of ruptured relationships are fortunate to be out of a stressful situation and they will be "better-off" over time. And sometimes they are.

These attitudes, now prevalent for more than 50 years, have both consciously and unconsciously justified an increasing recourse to separation and divorce. But are these justifications mere illusions? Early literature on the new divorce culture, largely written by relatively affluent and recently divorced women, celebrated the trend as liberating for both women and children. Perhaps it was for some women, but it was often a very different story as far as the children were concerned. In reality, many children bear a tragic cost. A troubling picture has emerged from studies of larger populations and from tracing the effects on children over time. It seems that there is rarely a trickle down of psychological benefits from mothers and fathers to their children. While statistically the majority of both men and women report that their lives are better after separating, the effects on children are less promising. By almost every measure, most children in divorced families have fared worse: emotional problems, early sexual experimentation, teen pregnancy, school truancy, delinquency and drug use are commonplace.

And re-marriage by the birth parents doesn't seem to be any kind of immunization from future problems. Children in step-families are even more likely to suffer emotional and behavioral problems, having difficulties with school and the police. Children of separated parents are more likely to carry emotional baggage, be occupationally aimless and have difficulty sustaining relationships even in early adulthood. Many psychologists believe that a parent's inability to sustain a relationship - that is so very important to a child - erodes the child's sense of identity, ability to trust and willingness to commit to a range of life experiences.

So, should couples stay together for the sake of the children? In some cases, the answer may be yes. There are qualifiers to that statement though. If the relationship involves persistent conflict and/or abuse or if the parties believe that solving deep differences is impossible and that maintaining the relationship will doom them to a life of misery, then it is obvious that separation is necessary and for the best. There is a valid argument that separation is less a tragedy than living in misery and teaching children the wrong things about relationships.

For those that are living in a relationship of tension, disagreements, boredom, emotional disconnection or even suffering within the experience of another romantic interest, there still could be great value in staying together. Choosing that option however, requires that they address the issues that brought them to the consideration of a separation in the first place. That may be through professional help or simply through solid hard relationship work. Whatever the approach, it is vital that any "cancer" within the relationship is treated.

It doesn't seem unreasonable that adults should be expected to sacrifice some of their own interests in order to preserve the stable and caring home necessary for the children that they helped bring into this world. If there is any chance a relationship can be sustained or repaired, surely parents have a responsibility to try. If there is no such chance, the parent still has a responsibility to make the children a priority by planning a life experience where their needs come first. One young Arizona couple, former high school sweet-hearts, found they were so different in adulthood that life together was impossible, but that somehow each was more tolerable when apart. But what of their daughter Carlee, aged four. The couple made a pact to remain involved in all aspects of the child's life, to share custody equally, to share costs fairly, to consult on all decisions, to deal with disagreements privately, to never disparage the other parent and to make life decisions that were consistently in the child's best interests. They lived by that agreement and the young girl flourished without any of the typical trauma associated with divorce. Carlee's experience may not be usual, but it does demonstrate that children can be a priority both within and out of the parental relationship. While perhaps more challenging, one doesn't need to live under the same roof in order to provide a loving, nurturing environment.

There are many people from previous generations that accepted a "shotgun marriage." The term is an obsolete phrase once used to describe a wedding triggered by an unplanned pregnancy. Changing attitudes, birth control strategies, legalized abortion and an increasing number of people cohabitating rather than getting married, have affected the number of people who feel pressured to marry because of an unplanned pregnancy. There are however still religious teachings that consider it a moral imperative. In the 1970's, twenty-seven percent of women with a premarital pregnancy experienced a "shotgun marriage" compared with just seven percent since the year 2000. That reduction is probably a good thing, given many people in "forced unions" later decide that the decision was a bad one. As in other separation situations, one of the primary considerations needs to be the welfare of any children. While not all un-planned pregnancies mean that marriage or cohabitating are based on pressure, it often is. If a child was originally planned and a time frame simply needed to be adjusted to accommodate an early birth, that is one matter, however partnership success is unlikely when a marriage or co-habitation are based on duress.

Another frequently asked question is whether or not married couples that are having difficulties should have a child in the hope that a new focus will rectify all that is wrong? It is not unusual for people who feel a loss of love and passion in their marriage, to think that if they have a child it will help improve the relationship. And sometimes it does. Couples who look at parenthood as an opportunity to grow emotionally may find themselves living with a renewed interest in making their relationship better along with that personal quest to be a better person. But often it doesn't. Studies report that up to 90 percent of couples say they are stressed, conflicted and less satisfied in their relationship after the birth of a baby and many of them "split." Statistically about 12 percent of relationships collapse by the time their "salvation" child is 18 months old.

Then there are those who choose to adopt a child. Adoption is a much more difficult experience than most people realize. Contrary to the often-stated adage, "love conquers all," it does not. Parents frequently find bonding more difficult than they expected and studies have shown that "adoption disruption" occurs in up to 20 percent of all adoptions. The older the child, the greater the chance of problems, with some studies reporting adoption dissolution at over 50 percent when other than a "new born" is involved. Multi-cultural adoptions have a similarly high dissolution rate. Although all of those decisions are never black and white in their outcomes, there is one truism and that is a belief that the addition of a child will change just about everything in a partnership. But very little of that "change" will make things easier, or will be likely to correct lingering problems.

So if you are considering leaving a forced "shotgun" marriage, or the addition of a child to a relationship, or to dissolve an existing relationship involving children, you really need to give those decisions some very serious second thought. Although many children carry the battle scars of their parent's separation into their adult life, it doesn't have to be so, and with the right approach it won't be.

Although you will feel intense anger in the early stages, do your children hear negative and disparaging comments about the other partner or the separation decision? Are discussions about any children held in private, stay focused and devoid of emotional outbursts? Do you spending private time with the children, letting them express thoughts and feelings without correction or criticism? If a child or childree spent time away with an "ex," do you ask only general questions like "did you have fun," avoiding any kind of inquisition? If you are seeing anyone new, do you avoid bringing them home until after you feel confident there may be some ongoing promise in the relationship. Most importantly, are you sensitive to your own thoughts, feelings and behaviours to the extent you to place your child's needs above your own.

EPILOGUE: *Choices & Statistics*

"If you love the life you live, you will live a life of love."
Unknown

Every single year, over a million of our neighbors will separate from an intimate relationship. Some as a result of abuse. There is a large commercial billboard that screams a message about domestic abuse. It reads simply **"*It's not your fault.*"** While it is true of course that the abused are not at fault – people only rarely choose abuse and death - the inference that a person could not have made different choices that might have prevented or dealt with the abuse differently, is simply not true.

Police officers see the result of domestic conflict almost daily. Dangerous, difficult situations that have escalated to the point of violence, injury and death. Conflict that has not just percolated over night, but deep interpersonal wounds, often festering for months and years before they erupt. Offences that have a "perpetrator" and a "victim," who both face significant pain and consequences. Actions that come from bad decisions. From their choices. Choices that under different circumstances might never have occurred.

But it is not trendy to speak of choices, decisions and accountability. We only speak of "victims." A victim is defined as a "person harmed, injured, or killed as a result of a crime, action or accident." Domestic violence is a crime and an action, but it is not an accident. It is purposeful on the part of the perpetrator and it might have been preventable if different choices had been made by both the perpetrator and the victim. But comments about *choices* are not fashionable to say the least and sacrilegious to say the worst. Why is that so? Perhaps because the words imply responsibility.

The notion of our experiences being unrelated to our choices is a common theme with many contemporary authors. Michelle Hodkin, best-selling author of the *Mara Dyer Trilogy* for example, writes: *"It isn't your fault. It's nothing you did. You cannot change who you are, any more than you can change black eyes to blue. You can only accept it. If you fight yourself, you will lose, and fighting leaves scars."* The truth is that we don't have to accept most things. Life is not about what happens to us, but rather how we choose to respond to what happens to us. If we change our choices, we will ultimately change what we experience and that will ultimately change who we are.

Let us consider a motor-vehicle collision for a moment. The public generally refers to them as accidents. But are they? An accident by definition is an event that happens by chance or that is without apparent or deliberate cause. Very few - if any- collisions are accidents. They are incidents. An incident is an event or occurrence resulting from an action. Most auto collisions result from an action – often from bad choices. Choices like drugs and alcohol, distraction, carelessness and so on. In most cases, automobile incidents could have been prevented or at least better dealt with by different decisions.

Such is the case when considering the question *"stay or go?"* What decisions could you have made that might have changed your life, might help you now or might change how you experience the future. Our choices will of course depend upon our scope of information and our level of consciousness. In other words, our choices depend on awareness and understanding of the things you have just learned about. Issues like:

- How do you tell real love from something else?
- Does he/she think differently than you do?
- How important is sex to both of you?
- Is a traditional marriage a good idea?
- Does your heritage matter?
- Does it matter that you come from different cultures?
- Does religion help or hinder you?
- What does a compatible partner look like?
- Why is money so often a problem?
- Why can't you communicate?

- Can anyone surmount infidelity?
- Can you cure an addict?
- What are the consequences for my children?
- How to stay in?
- How to get out?
- Where to find a new partner?
- What will determine my destiny?

Some relationships end early and probably should. Others end early and probably shouldn't. Some partnerships seem to last forever and should, others last a lifetime and probably shouldn't. Some unions never really flourish, while others bloom early and then die. Then there are those that destroy mind, body and soul. Relationships that are a result of choices.

For example:

- Only one third of partnerships are considered by the partners to be "happy," yet we they live with it until it worsens. Choices?
- The top reasons people separate are financial disagreements, poor communication and infidelity. Choices?
- It is estimated that up to 60 percent of married individuals will engage in infidelity at some point in their relationship. Choices?
- Over 75 percent of people who marry partners from an "affair" eventually divorce. Choices?

- A year after a divorce, 80 percent of men and 50 percent of women feel their lives are better. Choices?
- Many first relationship marriages end within the first ten years, with the average split occurring at eight years, perhaps after the proverbial "seven-year itch." Choices?
- The average age of couples that go through a first divorce is 30 years. Choices?
- The probability of a first marriage ending in a divorce within 5 years is 20 percent, but the probability of a premarital cohabitation breaking up within 5 years is 49 percent. After 10 years, the probability of a first marriage ending is 33 percent, compared with 62 percent for cohabitations. Choices?
- Women initiate over 75 percent of divorces. Choices?
- Couples who do divorce usually jump back into another relationship within 3 years. Choices?
- Couples who wait a minimum of 5 years before entering a second relationship are twice as likely to have a successful experience the second time around. Choices?
- Most men aren't considered ready for marriage until age 30 and those people that marry after 30 are far more likely to be married only once in their lifetime. Choices?

- People considered to be fundamentally religious have higher divorce rates than those that are considered more liberal. Choices?
- At the turn of the last century, 82 percent of marriages achieved 5-year anniversaries, 65 percent reached 10 years, 52 percent touched 15 years and 33 percent reached the celebrated 25th Anniversary. Choices?
- Dancers, bartenders and massage therapists have the highest rate of divorce of all professions while the clergy, optometrists and engineers have the lowest. Choices?
- Over twenty percent of women who divorce report domestic violence in the relationship – yet they remain there, often over a long period of time. Choices?

All of these experiences might have had a different outcome with better information, greater insight, personal support and of course, different choices.

AND MORE STATISTICS

If you live to be one hundred, you've got it made. Very few people die past that age."
George Burns

Comedian George Burns knew how to twist statistics and there are many others who do the same. Thoughtful people just urge caution on the interpretation of the numbers. Others might not use them at all. Author and humorist Mark Twain for example is quoted as saying "There are lies, damn lies and statistics." Sportscaster Vin Scully is even more cynical, "Statistics are used much like a drunk uses a lamppost; for support, not illumination." In summary, statistics may tell us nothing, they can be manipulated to say what we want them to say, or they can actually be informative.

To begin, let's acknowledge that the 50 % divorce rate number is in itself controversial because it is based on a simple calculation that takes the annual marriage rate per 1,000 people and compares that with the annual divorce rate. So, if there were 7.5 marriages per 1,000 people and 3.8 divorces, the rate would be about fifty percent.

Scientists say a preferred research method is to calculate how many specific people married, then divorced at a later date. Counted that way, the official rate has never exceeded 41 percent in the United States and 38 percent in Canada. Ten years ago many researchers predicted that a 50 percent figure would be exceeded within a few years, however statistically the divorce numbers began to drop after 2005. But that too is misleading. An increasing number of North Americans are no longer getting married, while "common law" unions and lone parent families are increasing. As a consequence, statistics about the ending of many relationships no longer appear in official statistics, whatever counting method is used.

Throughout the book there were many statistics, most from unnamed sources. They were taken primarily from government reports found within the U.S. Census Bureau and Statistics Canada, from studies at reputable North American Universities or from media reports (ie) Time magazine. Some of those numbers will amaze and they may even shock. Following are a few examples of findings that you might find surprising.

- The principle reason people get married is to formalize a commitment to another person, usually in response to a family or societal expectation.
- 58 percent of men who "cheat" claim to be happy in their marriages and more than 60 percent of affairs start at work.
- Divorce rates began to climb in the 1980's after some American States and the Canadian government passed legislation to allow "no-fault" divorces.
- There are now over 100 divorces every hour in North America.
- Only 86 percent of young people believe their current or future marriage will be successful.
- Twenty to thirty percent of women who divorce report domestic violence in the relationship.
- There are now more single person households in the U.S. and Canada than there are households with couples and children.

- Marriage and divorce rates are both reduced during times of economic recession. Marriages in the U.S. hit a forty year low in 2009.
- The average cost of a wedding in 2013 was $30,000.
- People who wait to marry after age 25 are almost 25 percent less likely to divorce - until they reach age 32.
- After age 32, the possibility of divorce for both genders increases by 5 percent annually.
- Most men aren't considered ready for marriage until age 30 and those people that marry after 30 are far more likely to be married only once in their lifetime.
- Panama City Florida is considered the U. S. Capital of divorce. Canada's is Calgary, Alberta.
- The annual divorce rate for same-sex couples is uncertain. Some studies report the rate is the same as that for "straight" partners while others report the rate is almost half.
- If parents appear to be happily married the risk of their children divorcing is reduced almost 15 percent.
- Since 1970, the lowest divorce rate in the U.S. occurred in 1981, with the highest rate in 2005.
- In 2014, twenty percent of Americans had never been married, in contrast with only ten

percent in 1960. The number of women never married was about five percent less than men.
- Sweden has the highest rate of divorce at 55 percent and India the lowest at 1 percent. Australia, the United Kingdom and most European countries report between 40 and 45 percent, except for Mediterranean countries like Greece, Spain and Italy where divorce rates are less than half that of their neighbors.
- About half of the people in countries like India and Pakistan believe that divorce is morally unacceptable compared with 22 percent in the United States and 9 percent in Canada. Only 4 percent of Spaniards, the lowest percentage in the world, hold that view.

This book was about life conditions that need to be carefully examined when considering the monumental decision of whether to continue in a relationship or move on. There are times in which ending a relationship may be inevitable and the "right" thing to do. There are often warning signs and while partners may be able to overcome serious risk factors with determination and help from others, they will as often as not, end in separation.

So how does one ultimately decide whether or not to stay in a relationship? While there are obviously no hard and fast rules, there are a few considerations that tend to help. Firstly, one needs to look at what exists within the relationship. On the positive side of the "balance sheet," in no particular order are the requirements for trust, honesty, good communication, safety, shared interests, helpfulness, kindness, respect, common goals, money attitudes, earning potential, fidelity and a strong commitment to the relationship. On the negative side of the ledger there is dishonesty, distrust, abuse, harshness, disrespect, dread, addiction, laziness, poverty, infidelity and a low commitment to the relationship.

In addition to looking at the journal of assets and liabilities, it is important to look at whose needs may be influencing the decision. In a decision this important, it is crucial that the ramifications the choice will have on others are balanced with one's own desires. While it is a mistake to forgo most or all of one's own needs in favor of the children or partner, it is equally a mistake to consider only one's own self and ignore the unavoidable impact on the family.

If you have not yet made a decision, you might wish to review some of the most important indicators detailed throughout the book. The first indicator or "warning" sign is a difference in the level of commitment to the relationship. Commitment means how much each partner desires a future together, how strongly he or she believes the two partners are on the same team and how much he or she is willing to sacrifice or give to the partner. Disagreements about money are often central to this commitment or lack of it.

The second warning sign is reflected in verbal and non-verbal communication that is aggressive and hurtful. Aggression is always dangerous as it indicates deep underlying anger and difficulty managing conflict and emotions. When aggression is coupled with behavior that is aimed at controlling a companion, the partnership is unlikely to survive.

The third warning sign is early relationship infidelity. Though many behaviors and norms have changed over the years, most people still expect sexual faithfulness in their relationships. Although a single transgression may be forgotten or at least forgiven, it is statistically likely to be repeated and then is likely not to be forgiven.

The fourth warning sign is addictive behavior. Whether the addiction is to a substance or an experience, whether it is to alcohol, drugs, sex, gambling, shopping or work, the prognosis for a relationship is poor without professional intervention. A partnership can simply not survive within an atmosphere that places a priority on the addiction and is often shrouded in deceit.

Although there are many situations where these four difficult challenges have been addressed successfully, in most cases the long-term history of success is generally not good. There are many other possible challenges within a relationship that are outside of these four most troublesome indicators of relationship collapse, but many if not most of them can be rectified with understanding, commitment and persistence.

At the beginning of this book a hope was expressed that this work would be of some help in making a *"stay or go"* decision. While it is now time to complete the decision grid found as an appendix, the truth is that you probably already know the answer. As your brain processed the information through the books pages, you will have intuitively concluded what you need to do. Think about it. The subconscious mind knows what the soul wants. Best wishes!

There is little science in the following framework, but if you want a little validation for your feelings and the conclusion you just arrived at, complete the following grid.

APPENDIX: *A decision grid*

DIRECTIONS
1. Read through the list of issues, select the top 5 of most importance to you and print X 2 in the "WEIGHT" column next to each selection. Print X 1 in the remaining "weight" boxes.
2. Reflecting on each Chapter, use the score boxes and answer the 23 questions on a scale of 1 to 5 with 1 being "not at all," 3 being "somewhat" and 5 being "very much."
3. Multiply your rating by 2 for each of the 5 priority items identified in point # 1 above and place those numbers in the "score" column. The remaining "scores" stay the same.
4. Total the score column. There is a potential of 140 points. Score less than 50% (70) and your answer may be obvious. Score between 50% (70) and 80% (112) and you might want to work harder. Score over 80% (112 to 140) and leaving could be a big mistake.

#	ISSUES	WEIGHT	QUESTION	SCORE	TOTAL
1	Love		Am I still attracted, attached and feel assurance about our future together?		
2	Sex		Do we talk about our feelings and do I still enjoy sex?		
3	Obsolescence		Do I still feel close, physically and mentally within this relationship?		

4	Searching		Do we still have compatible interests, values and energy?			
5	Personality		Do I still appreciate and enjoy my partner's personality type?			
6	Homosexuality		Is my sexual orientation accepted and honored?			
7	Heredity		Is our heredity compatible and enriching?			
8	Energy		Am I comfortable with my partner's energy?			
9	Consciousness		Do I use strategies to reduce stress and increase my sensitivity?			
10	Destiny		Do I understand that my decisions are determining my results?			
11	Gender		Do I accept my partner's differences without trying to change them?			
12	Geography		Does where we live positively affect our relationship?			
13	Culture		Are our cultures compatible?			
14	Religion		Is my religion/spirituality supportive without judgement?			

15	Laws		Do I know the laws that I must consider?		
16	Money		Do we have compatible values about income and spending?		
17	Infidelity		Is his/her infidelity surmountable?		
18	Communication		Do we communicate openly, clearly and honestly?		
19	Addiction		Can I overcome his/her addictions?		
20	Illness		Can I accept and live with his/her illness?		
21	Aging		Do I recognize the limitations of my age?		
22	Bedlam		Can I handle the chaos that comes with separation/divorce?		
23	Children		Will our children be ok?		

THE AUTHOR

Prior to his retirement, Ronald A. LaJeunesse had more than thirty-years experience in the education, health and criminal justice systems. Educated in psychiatric nursing, counseling psychology, education and business administration at the Universities of Saskatchewan, Alberta and Calgary, the author received appointments as the Executive Director (ED) of the Canadian Mental Health Association in Alberta, ED of the Mental Health Branch and CEO of the Mental Health Board of the Government of Alberta. He also taught in the Saskatchewan Department of Health and at Mount Royal College. He served as the elected Chairman of a large school Board, as a Police Commissioner overseeing the work of a major urban police service, served as Deputy-Mayor in a municipal government and chaired the Board of a Spiritual Centre. In addition, he did individual and family counseling in community clinics, owned and managed a franchised restaurant and led a human services research and consulting company. The recipient of numerous professional and public service awards including two Governor Generals medals for community service, he has presented at international conferences and written three previous books, one receiving the province of Alberta's top literary award.

Outside of his addiction to work, Ron experienced a life threatening and debilitating injury while playing hockey. He helped raise four sons and a child who was a government ward and astoundingly somehow sustained more than a fifty-year relationship. What he learned through his professional career, through his disability, through community involvements, through his family and friends, through subject research including nation-wide interviews, from his own struggle with "stay or go," but mostly from his partner Wendy, has provided the fodder for this book.

This work is dedicated to my life partner, lover, friend, mentor and soulmate. Like all others, our relationship has had highs and lows. Fortunately for me, that life partner has demonstrated with the greatest of love, wisdom and skill, that it is not the gravity of the problems, but the caring, perseverance and quality of the solving effort that determines the outcome. To Wendy Carol, I am eternally grateful.

Made in the USA
Columbia, SC
13 November 2023